A publication of

NATIONAL ALLIANCE OF BUSINESS

The National Alliance of Business was founded in 1968 by President Lyndon B. Johnson and Henry Ford II. They believed that our nation's social and economic problems could best be tackled by a unique collaboration between business and government. NAB's initial charge was to hire and train thousands of young Americans, particularly the most disadvantaged, during a critical turning point in this nation's history. Since its inception, NAB has focused on building effective partnerships between the public and private sectors nationwide. NAB's mission today is to support America's business leadership in committing its energy and capabilities to solving the most important issues of our time—issues related to the quality of this country's education system, workforce, and job-training programs.

Using Quality
to Redesign
School Systems

Peggy Siegel and Sandra Byrne

Foreword by
David T. Kearns

Using Quality to Redesign School Systems

The Cutting Edge of Common Sense

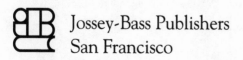

Jossey-Bass Publishers
San Francisco

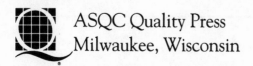

ASQC Quality Press
Milwaukee, Wisconsin

Funding for this study was provided by The Pew Charitable Trusts, The
Joyce Foundation, and the Office of Educational Research and Improvement in the U.S. Department of Education.

For sales outside the United States, contact Maxwell Macmillan
International Publishing Group, 866 Third Avenue, New York,
New York 10022.

Manufactured in the United States of America. Nearly all Jossey-Bass
books, jackets, and periodicals are printed on recycled paper that
contains at least 50 percent recycled waste, including 10 percent post-
consumer waste. Many of our materials are also printed with vegetable-
based ink; during the printing process these inks emit fewer volatile
organic compounds (VOCs) than petroleum-based inks. VOCs contribute to the formation of smog.

The epigraph at the beginning of the book is from Phillip C. Schlechty's
Schools for the 21st Century: Leadership Imperatives for Educational Reform, p. xvi.
Copyright 1990 by Jossey-Bass Inc., Publishers. Reprinted with permission.

Library of Congress Cataloging-in-Publication Data

Siegel, Peggy M.
  Using quality to redesign school systems : the cutting edge of
common sense / Peggy Siegel, Sandra Byrne.
      p.   cm.
  A joint publication in the Jossey-Bass education series and the
Jossey-Bass management series.
  Includes bibliographical references and index.
  ISBN 1-55542-649-2
  1. School management and organization—United States.   2. Total
quality management—United States.   3. Industry and education—
United States   I. Byrne, Sandra, date.   II. Title.
III. Series: Jossey-Bass education series.   IV. Series: Jossey-Bass
management series.
LB2805.S5874   1994
371.2'00973—dc20   93-40965
                                                                  CIP

FIRST EDITION
HB Printing   10 9 8 7 6 5 4 3 2 1   *Code 9443*

Contents

Foreword

In the next ten years, America's schools will go through tremendous change. The requirements of an increasingly demanding work environment and world economy will drive vast improvements in the ways we teach and learn. The success of our communities and schools in *managing* this change will determine our ability to compete—as individuals, as businesses, and as a nation—in the twenty-first century.

I got involved in education, not out of some esoteric concern, but as a businessman. At Xerox, we were fighting to stay in business, and I was worried that we would not have a workforce with the skills needed to meet the demands of competition. It became clear that education is a fundamental underpinning to our nation's competitiveness and the solution to a whole set of challenges America faces, and that if we were to compete, as a company and as a nation, we would have to dramatically change our schools.

The bottom line is that most of our schools are not up to the task. I am not one who bashes our schools or laments the problems we face. The overwhelming conclusion of my tenure at the Department of Education is that America has some of the best teachers and administrators I have ever seen. The problem is that despite their dedication and innovation, school *systems* remain slow to change—slow to react to the demands of an increasingly technical and competitive world.

School systems are institutions that, like many others, are not conducive to change. I learned at Xerox that change is oner-ous—it affects the organizations and people we have grown accustomed to. Many of us fear change, since it destabilizes our lives and breaks the status quo. But change is also inevitable and constant, and so our ability to embrace and *manage* change becomes our ability to succeed in the future. All of this is cer-tainly true of our school bureaucracies: they are as entrenched as any institution in America, and yet their ability to manage change will determine our ability to compete in the twenty-first century.

Quality is an important part of the *process* of managing such institutional change. It involves the tools we give all of our people to do their job. Quality is not the end—it is the means. It requires a change in culture and in operations. And while the operations and outputs of schools are clearly different from those of most companies, the lessons of change in corporate America and the processes applied are invaluable to our educa-tion system.

Using Quality to Redesign School Systems documents some of those lessons and processes already at work in companies and school systems across America. This book should serve as a valu-able resource to those serious about redesigning education sys-tems and addressing many of the critical issues our principals, teachers, and administrators face every day. It is not intended as a definitive "how-to" but as a reference source of what has worked well elsewhere.

This book also helps to define the role of the business community. During my travels with the Department of Educa-tion, the one thing I urged businesspeople to do was to support the educators and community leaders willing to take risks and embrace change. This book outlines specific ways to do just that. It serves as a challenge to encourage and *actively* support sys-temic change. And I am pleased that the National Alliance of Business is taking a leadership role in establishing this new era of business-education partnerships. Our children deserve the best schools in the world, uniquely American and unique to each community. Our task as citizens and as business leaders is to help education professionals bring about this change.

January 1994   David T. Kearns,
                                                        former chairman and CEO
                                                        of Xerox Corporation and
                                                        former deputy secretary of the
                                                        U.S. Department of Education

Preface

Since its founding in 1968, the National Alliance of Business (NAB) has focused on one primary mission: helping America work. Increasingly, the task requires the combined commitment, talents, and actions of both the public and the private sector. It requires a communitywide effort. And it must engage policymakers at all levels of government.

Lifelong learning is at the heart of helping America work and is required of each of us and of every organization. In such a learning environment, who teaches whom is less important than that everyone learn. The philosophy, practices, and tools of Total Quality Management (TQM) promise to help all of us address our lifelong learning needs together, whether at school, at work, or at home—as part of a community.

As you will read in *Using Quality to Redesign School Systems*, TQM is a revolutionary, transformational process that represents wrenching change. The private sector is just beginning to apply its tenets; an estimated 15 percent of businesses are practicing TQM. For those who are, the benefits are enormous. Our study suggests that the public sector—in this case, educators—can successfully apply comparable principles and practices to reap those same benefits.

In conducting the study that forms the basis of this book, NAB visited seven educational institutions that have made excellent starts in transforming themselves into high-performance organizations. We looked at their institutional and human characteristics, believing there was much to be learned from their experiences. These findings should contribute to the discussions directed at reforming the $257 billion education industry.

I especially want to thank the team that planned this project, spent a year on the road interviewing all of the sites, and wrote this book—Peggy Siegel, for coming up with the idea that led to this project and for the research design, and Sandra Byrne, for demonstrating the best personal attributes of Quality on a daily basis through interactions with her NAB colleagues and customers. In their roles as "human camcorders," Siegel and Byrne captured for business leaders the organizational and political realities confronting educators who are making important changes, often in the face of untenable odds.

If NAB has done a good job of conveying the information in this book, companies that have reinvented themselves through TQM will be motivated to help school systems do the same. Once they understand the challenges educators encounter and the valuable resources they have within their ranks, companies will want to act not because NAB encourages them to, but because their own enlightened self-interest as business leaders representing their communities drives them to. Once they have made that commitment, business leaders can look to the Alliance for support. This publication, we hope, will serve as a useful starting point.

January 1994   William Kolberg,
                                              president and CEO of the
                                              National Alliance of Business

Acknowledgments

Conducting over 200 interviews in eleven sites enabled us to collect a wealth of information. In no way could we ever report the totality of their Total Quality efforts. What we set out to do was to capture the "human spirit" that resides in these high-performing work environments. Hopefully, the illustrations of TQM applications, although limited in space, do them justice. By documenting the experiences of these particular sites, we hope to reinforce their efforts and improve their odds for success. By sharing their experiences with others, we hope to swell their ranks by encouraging additional business and education leaders to join them in initiating comparable change efforts.

Many individuals deserve our appreciation for contributing to this book. First, we express our deeply felt respect and gratitude to those at the eleven sites we visited—respect for what they are accomplishing and gratitude for enabling us to record it. NAB is indebted to Marc Tucker and the National Center on Education and the Economy for "loaning us" John Foley and Norman Deets, two former Xerox executives who teamed with us on most of our site visits and served as key advisers to the project. Norm and John personified the best attributes of Quality and teamwork and reinforced NAB's commitment to bringing business and education leaders together on systemic change issues.

On a personal note, after spending such a long time together on the road, we cannot think of two other people who would have worn as well. We also want to thank John for coining the subtitle of this publication, which is a tribute to both his creativity and his common sense. We gratefully acknowledge the 200 individuals who agreed to talk with us, including our primary contacts at each of the eleven sites: John Kelsch (Xerox); Ed Bales (Motorola); Marsha Taylor (Globe Metallurgical); John West and Jean Ward Jones (Federal Express); David Gangel (Rappahannock County Public Schools); Ed Kelly and Den Boyd (Prince William County Public Schools); Chuck Melvin, David Romstad, Linda Barrows, and Steve Ashmore (Southwestern Wisconsin Consortium); Larrae Rocheleau (Mt. Edgecumbe High School); Lewis Rappaport and Franklin Schargel (George Westinghouse Vocational and Technical High School); Rick Mills and Chip Evans (Vermont Department of Education); and Verel Salmon (Millcreek Township School District). Credit for what they are doing belongs to the eleven sites. Responsibility for any "defects" in reporting what they are doing, however, rests with us.

In particular, we want to express our admiration for David Kearns, former CEO of Xerox, and the students at Mt. Edgecumbe High School in Sitka, Alaska. Perhaps more than anyone, they represent the "alpha" and "omega" of Quality. David Kearns embodies the leadership qualities it takes to transform a system. The Mt. Edgecumbe students demonstrate why it is worth the effort.

Sue Tucker, Education Director at GOAL/QPC, gave us liberal access to her organization's glossary of Quality terms and tools prepared specifically for educators. Curt Reimann, director of the Malcolm Baldrige National Quality Award Office, gave us liberal access to his insights about reinforcing Quality in different types of settings. We thank each of them for their considerable contributions.

We would also like to thank key members of NAB's own staff—Steve Mitchell, for his thoughtful reactions to and input on the first draft; Patty Mitchell and Esther Schaeffer, for their advice throughout this project; Bill Kolberg, Pierce Quinlan, Ron Gunn, and Foster Smith—as well as Patty Mitchell and Esther Schaeffer—for their feedback on the first draft; Iris

Moore, Rosalyn Johnson, and Bernice Jones, for administrative support; Maureen Bozell, for editing the draft; and Brenda Bell, for introducing the manuscript to Jossey-Bass and the American Society of Quality Control, our co-publishers.

This book could not have been written without generous funding and support from The Pew Charitable Trusts. We are also deeply indebted to The Joyce Foundation and the Office of Educational Research and Improvement in the U.S. Department of Education, which helped fund the research.

Finally, since learning what we did from those we interviewed proved to be a lot more fun than writing it all down, we would like to thank the music of the great composers (Sandra) and Bruce Springsteen (Peggy) for making a labor-intensive task a little less intense.

Washington, D.C.   Peggy Siegel
January 1994   Sandra Byrne

*This book is dedicated to
our friend Norman Deets,
who always saw the best in others
as he gave the best of himself.*

The Authors

Peggy Siegel is vice president for business/education projects at the National Alliance of Business (NAB). She received her B.A. degree (1968) in social science as a Phi Beta Kappa graduate of Ohio State University, where she also received her M.A. degree (1972) in political science and her Ph.D. degree (1974), with honors, in education administration. Before joining NAB, she was a management consultant with Towers/Perrin and Pelavin and Associates, specializing in educational governance, organization, and operational issues.

Siegel has more than twenty years of experience working in, consulting for, analyzing, and writing about state and local education systems. She served as a senior staff person in the Ohio General Assembly and director of state governmental relations for the Cuyahoga County (Cleveland) Board of Commissioners. At the National Conference of State Legislatures, she managed a program that provided education policy analysis and technical assistance to legislatures nationwide. At NAB, Siegel directs projects that forge business-education partnerships around systemic change issues. In 1993, she was selected as an examiner for the Malcolm Baldrige National Quality Award.

Sandra Byrne is senior project manager at NAB, where she has management responsibilities for various business-education partnership programs, including quality management and school-to-work transition. She earned her B.S. (1967) and M.Ed. (1968) degrees at the University of Illinois in elementary education. Byrne spent ten years as a classroom teacher in elementary and special education, followed by five years managing projects and providing technical assistance as an education specialist at the Illinois Department of Education and the Mid-Atlantic Regional Resource Center. She also spent several years working in the private sector.

Using Quality
to Redesign
School Systems

School leaders, like business leaders,
must come to understand that if America's
schools are to meet the needs of the
twenty-first century, then—like America's
corporate structure—they must be reinvented.

Phillip C. Schlechty
Schools for the 21st Century

Chapter 1

Introduction

Recently, numerous U.S. companies have had to rethink and
revise the nature of work—what gets done, how, when, for
whom, and by whom—not because they have wanted to, but
because they have had to in order to survive. Many companies
are succeeding, but some are not.

Today's educators confront an even greater challenge.
They must design and oversee a system that maximizes opportunities for all students to achieve. Not just one company's survival, but that of the entire society is at stake. We cannot afford
to have our educators fail. But they need broad-based community and political support in order to succeed. The National
Alliance of Business (NAB) believes that successful companies
have a valuable resource to contribute to the current education
reform agenda. Companies can share the experiences, pain,
and wisdom of their own restructuring initiatives, often from
hindsight.

Unfortunately, this sharing of common experiences is no
easy task. The organizational and cultural landscapes of business and education appear to be worlds apart. But it does not
have to be this way.

In 1991–92, NAB secured funding to explore the potential of Total Quality Management (also known as Total Quality,

Quality Management, or simply Quality—or TQM for short) for reaching common ground. We wanted to discover, firsthand, how business and education leaders were using TQM to transform their respective organizations. Based on their experiences, we wanted to assess whether and how TQM could be employed as a comprehensive change strategy in redesigning education organizations so they could improve student and system performance. Finally, we wanted to determine how business and education leaders using Quality practices could work together, in Schlechty's words, to reinvent American education.

Why Should Educators Care About Quality?

Conversations about applying Quality in education should not begin with Quality, the means to an end. They need to begin with the end itself, improving learning.

Defining the Need: Improving Learning

Economic realities dictate that all children must be prepared to be lifelong learners. Increasingly, educators are committing themselves to this essential goal. The challenge, however, is not only committing to it, but figuring out how to accomplish it.

The primary objective of the current education restructuring movement is to improve learning. Improved learning generally means that all students, by the time they graduate from high school, will have a solid command of *basic academic skills* (that is, reading, writing, and computation); *foundation skills* that are both content related (such as English, mathematics, science, history, and geography) and work related (for example, listening, speaking, and working in teams); and *value-added skills*, such as capabilities in the areas of leadership, problem solving, and creativity. Schools, in essence, provide students with the knowledge, skills, and opportunity to become lifelong learners.

The key relationships in restructuring education are the ones between students and those with whom they interact most closely: their teachers, parents, and peers. Seen in this light, learning is a shared responsibility and is the chief product of these relationships. Learning also is affected greatly by the larger organizational context in which it occurs. Therefore, the efforts of students, teachers, and parents to focus on the dynamics of learning must be reinforced by the education system in which learning takes place.

Setting rigorous student performance standards and using multiple assessments to evaluate how well students meet those standards are critical elements of improving learning. But adopting higher standards and richer assessments alone will not result in success. The collective will, activities, and resources of the entire organization also must be directed toward improving learning.

School systems must have the *organizational capacity* to determine how they can work with students to meet higher standards. They must have the organizational capacity to collect, analyze, and use data to improve student and system performance. And they must have the organizational capacity to deploy resources and track progress over time in accomplishing priorities. In other words, the management processes — both instructional and noninstructional — that collectively form the education system must be aligned to support learning.

The scarcity of public dollars also is driving educators to maximize efficiency in managing their organizations. Tolerating lack of productivity in school systems, just as assuredly as tolerating failure in students, is no longer a viable option.

At issue is the following question: What is the best way to ensure that all students (regardless of individual need or talent) and schools (regardless of wealth) have the chance to succeed? Policymakers and educators need evidence of what organizational structures and processes are most likely to yield success for all students. To be able to target their human and financial assets more effectively on learning, they also need the opportunity to identify and address the root causes of organizational inefficiencies throughout the system.

Addressing the Need: Organizational Capacity

TQM is value added in education because it represents a comprehensive, systemic approach to making improvements. Quality gives stakeholders the ways and means to judge each reform initiative within a larger organizational context. It can build on what is working in education and what educators hold dear. Reinforc-

ing educators to lead their systems—and their ability to make
continuous improvements over time—also is far preferable to
the current crisis-driven, ad hoc state of education decision making. Seen in this light, the ability to define, analyze, and redesign
the education system is *essential* for sustaining restructuring
efforts targeted at student and organizational performance.

     Addressing isolated elements of the nation's education cri-
sis—teaching, curriculum, assessment, and so on—has proved
at best only minimally successful in improving America's school
systems. Thus, increasing numbers of educators are becoming
convinced that the school system itself needs to be redesigned.
They recognize that substance and process issues must become
joined as part of the same restructuring agenda. And they are
willing to lead the change effort. But these innovators need the
organizational capacity to make change happen. Thus, what
Quality offers education—as will become apparent in the subsequent pages of this book—is a way to piece together the various
fabrics of current education restructuring initiatives into a systemic "whole cloth." In essence, Quality *connects the dots.*

Our Intended Customers; or, Who Should Read This Book

Our study was designed to fill a missing link—the juncture
between business and education—in the rapidly expanding
Quality literature. It therefore focuses on how TQM as a management philosophy translates into practice, both in school systems and in corporations. This book also is intended to prompt
action. We want to motivate three primary audiences—business
leaders, education leaders, and government leaders—who
together can create and sustain the momentum for comprehensive change in education.

Business Leaders

First and foremost, we want to activate business leaders to do
something about what is happening in American schools. Many
realize that the survival of their own companies, as well as the economic well-being of their communities, depends on citizens who
think, work, and participate. We especially hope to reach those
who have used Quality practices to make their own companies

more successful and therefore have a valuable resource—their experiences—to share with educators. Our target audience also includes business leaders willing to learn about education systems so they can reinforce the more arduous journeys of their public sector colleagues. And this book is aimed at business leaders wise enough to view partnerships as an equal playing field— because they will undoubtedly learn something of value to bring back to their own companies from such experiences.

Education Leaders

We also want to reinforce the efforts of education leaders committed to serving all students well and who understand that the education system, as it currently operates, is incapable of accomplishing this challenging goal. These are educators who, having become convinced of the need to change, are now looking for practical solutions. Many are risk takers and currently are creating—or would like to create—a new type of education system, one targeted at the needs of all children. We want to reinforce education leaders who are restructuring their organizations and see the benefit of employing Quality processes, not in competition with, but complementary to promising change efforts already underway. Many education leaders, eager to engage successful businesses and ultimately the entire community in their change efforts, perceive TQM as a means to that end. In short, we hope to reach education leaders who, by sharing their experiences, can provide their colleagues with much-needed "change" models.

Government Leaders

Finally, we want to encourage government leaders who are convinced that education systems must change. We hope the book will aid policymakers searching for ways to turn the rhetoric of systemic change into reality, even if such actions run counter to the ways education policy currently is made and school systems are governed in this country.

Admittedly, in addressing these three distinct audiences, we walk a precarious tightrope. Based on respective comfort levels, their priorities and strategies regarding educational improvement may diverge. For example, most business leaders will feel more at home using TQM to analyze noninstructional operations. In contrast, most educators will want to focus their change efforts on instructional areas—the heartbeat of education—particularly operations that directly affect the classroom. Most policymakers, in turn, probably could care less about work processes, instructional or noninstructional. They want information on results—on whether school systems are improving student performance—not on what they are doing and how they are doing it.

The information presented in this book should help bridge the differences among these three important groups. Quality practices have the potential to forge a seamless alliance among them in ways that address their individual concerns. The contents of the book are meant to bring the parties together. Only together will they be able to redesign our education system to generate the learning that we desire and that our children so richly deserve.

Why This Book: Five Key Questions Asked and Answered

During the two years since NAB first conceptualized and conducted this study, interest in TQM has escalated rapidly in education circles. For example, over 600 individuals have joined a Total Quality Network, created by the American Association of School Administrators. W. Edwards Deming (universally celebrated as having helped Japan restore its post–World War II economy by focusing on Quality Management) has prepared a series of tapes and lectures designed especially for educators. A number of states, such as New York, Florida, Texas, Minnesota, North Carolina, and South Carolina, have formulated or are interested in developing their own versions of the National Quality (Baldrige) Award.[1] At this writing, the federal government appears on the verge of extending the Baldrige Award to

---

[1]The Malcolm Baldrige National Quality Award was created in Public Law 100–107 by Congress in 1987 and is administered by the National Institute of Standards and Technology within the U.S. Department of Commerce. Its purpose is to improve the quality and productivity of American companies. Between 1988 and 1993, nineteen award winners have been selected, representing manufacturing and service companies and small businesses.

education and health care. And the professional education journals are replete with advertisements announcing conferences, publications, quality experts and trainers, and videos designed to assist educators in implementing TQM.

Clearly, many educators are eager to learn about Quality. They especially want to know more about who is doing what and how. This book is intended to address their concerns. Based on the experiences of business and education leaders who are exercising Quality decision making with Quality tools in Quality environments, we intend to answer five key questions:

1. *What is Quality—in practice?* Much has been written about TQM and is readily available. It need not be repeated here. Our objective instead is to move beyond the conceptual to the "actual." Chapter One introduces the eleven sites in our study—the four companies and the seven education sites—and summarizes the reasons for their selection. Chapter Two offers several definitions of TQM, but its ultimate objective is to illustrate the ways that business and education leaders at these sites define Quality through their practice of it.

2. *How is Quality being implemented?* Our objective in answering this question is to provide a "missing link." All too often the "what's" of successful change efforts are shared without the "how's." In contrast, we want to give the reader a sense of the different contexts of change. Chapter Three, therefore, provides mini case studies of how three of these sites are implementing Quality, the challenges they face, and the choices they are making in altering the ways they do business. Chapter Four analyzes the *change process itself,* by summarizing common key decision points in the implementation strategies from all eleven sites.

3. *What are educators doing to apply Quality?* The proof, for true believers and skeptics alike, of TQM's value for education will be in the practice and in the results. Thus, in determining the contents of this book, we asked numerous educators what information on Quality would be most helpful to them. The overwhelming response was: "Make TQM real for us." Chapter Five, the longest chapter, illus-

trates the different ways educators in our study are applying Quality tools and processes. The information is presented in vignettes that illustrate what individuals using
TQM in educational settings do, how they do it, and what
they say about it.

These real-world examples are organized under the
seven categories of the Malcolm Baldrige National Quality
Award: (1) Leadership, (2) Information and Analysis,
(3) Strategic Quality Planning, (4) Human Resource
Development and Management, (5) Management of
Process Quality, (6) Quality and Operational Results, and
(7) Customer Focus and Satisfaction. Increasing numbers
of educators are applying similar Quality criteria to assess
their own organizations. Therefore, the examples contained in Chapter Five should prove "user friendly,"
enabling educators to compare their own practices against
the successful practices of others. In addition, many companies use the Baldrige Criteria for their internal use, as
an organizational self-assessment tool. Consequently, the
examples presented in this study should make education
operations less enigmatic to business leaders, thereby reinforcing the collaborations between public and private sector created to improve student and system performance.

4. *What are the critical challenges in implementing Quality in education?* Chapter Six recaps the similarities in applying
Quality practices in business and education. Most critically, it identifies the additional challenges of customizing
TQM to an education setting. Before education and business leaders can work together to improve student and system performance, bridges of understanding must be built.
The basic message to business leaders is: Know what you
are up against. As tough as the road has been in transforming your own company with TQM, be prepared for
an even bumpier ride in education.

5. *What can business do to help?* Having laid down the
gauntlet to business leaders, we would be remiss if we
did not offer some options on what they can do to help
educators improve their systems. NAB's primary objective,
after all, is to forge lasting partnerships between business

and education that can overcome the barriers. Consequently, Chapter Seven offers advice to business. We want
to tap into business leaders' realm of enlightened self-
interest—so that those who read this book will see opportunities to assist educators in restructuring their school systems and so that education leaders will be able to identify
leverage points where business can help. If business leaders have been successful in transforming their own companies using TQM and if they have read this far, this book is
intended to incite them to action.

Key Findings and Observations

Eleven site visits and over 200 interviews have led us to four key
findings, which are amplified in subsequent chapters. These
observations should encourage business leaders who wish to
align with educators in advancing Quality as a systemic change
strategy in education.

> *Finding 1:* Quality as a comprehensive, systemic
> change strategy is applicable to an education
> setting.

Like the business leaders in the companies we visited, the
educators we interviewed are committed to and involved in
transforming their organizations, using Quality principles, processes, and practices as the driving force. In essence, they recognize the need to build an infrastructure that supports systemic reform and continuous improvement and are using
Quality to do it. And like their business counterparts, many of
these education leaders have adopted and adapted key Quality
components to the realities of their respective organizations.

> *Finding 2:* Implementing Quality in education is
> not a quick fix; in fact, it will be even more difficult
> than in the private sector.

Successful companies, even Baldrige Award winners, are
never completely "TQMed." There simply is no finish line to con-

tinuous improvement. At a minimum, however, certain conditions must be present for Quality to take root: united, committed leadership; a trusting, collaborative culture; ample training resources; flexible use of time; definable work processes tied to strategic goals; identifiable customers, suppliers, and organizational boundaries; availability and use of customer information to make good decisions and track progress; as well as the capability to reward success and correct deficiencies. Unfortunately, these same conditions that many successful companies take as givens are rare occurrences in education environments.

Certain conditions also must be present before Quality can be institutionalized. TQM is "for real" when the practices, processes, and tools are no longer an add-on program or fad but become part and parcel of how an organization does business. It is for real when change efforts continue, despite the turnover of key "change agents." Few, if any, school systems have reached this stage in their transition to becoming Quality-driven organizations. *Whether Quality will have the staying power to help educators restructure school systems is, in fact, the central issue raised by this study.*

Finding 3: Business management experience and political support are critical—if not essential—resources for implementing Quality in education.

Educators who have taken the lead in implementing Quality have succeeded in spite of, rather than because of, their organizations. By exercising leadership, the educators in this study have created a Quality oasis and the genesis of a supportive culture. This country needs them and others like them to succeed. But acting alone, educators can rarely generate the organizational capacity needed to make continuous improvements over time.

Even where TQM is being implemented successfully in education, efforts appear too fragile to survive the turnover of key leaders. The will to change the education system from the inside needs to be bolstered by influential voices on the outside. As a key customer of education, private sector leaders must play a vital role in supporting public sector leaders. Business can be a persistent force for change and a reliable source of information and support. Business-education collaborations can serve as the fulcrum for initiating and sustaining student and system improvement efforts.

> *Finding 4:* Before business and education leaders can use Quality together to restructure education, bridges between them need to be built.

Our study provides insights into the kinds of barriers that must be overcome before business and education leaders can join forces to improve education. For one, the public and private sectors remain wary of each other. The relevance of business practices and principles to education operations may not be immediately apparent, although many school systems are among the largest employers in their respective communities. Some school boards, administrators, and teachers voice open hostility to business approaches ("We don't produce widgets; we deal with students!"). In turn, many business leaders lack an adequate command of the context in which school systems operate ("Why can't educators just produce results? Everything is 'process'!"). A fundamental constraint in creating successful partnerships between the public and private sectors is simply getting the parties to sit down and talk.

As a first step to bridging the barriers, organizations need a way to engage in constructive dialogue. This holds true for units within the same institution. And it certainly is true across different institutions. Quality practices and tools can meet that need. They provide a common language and a common decision-making lens for education, government, and business leaders so they can begin a much-needed conversation. Hopefully, the contents of this study will encourage them to gather at the table and will give them some issues to discuss.

Whom We Saw and Why

This section briefly describes the eleven sites we visited during 1992 in conducting this study. The following list of sites includes four companies and seven education sites—one state department of education, two schools, three school districts, and one interdistrict collaboration.

Business

Xerox
Motorola
Globe Metallurgical
Federal Express

Education

Rappahannock County Public Schools, Virginia
Prince William County Public Schools, Virginia
Mt. Edgecumbe High School, Alaska
Southwestern Wisconsin Quality Consortium
Vermont Department of Education
George Westinghouse Vocational and Technical High
    School, Brooklyn, New York
Millcreek Township School District, Pennsylvania

Business Sites

In 1987, Congress created the Malcolm Baldrige National Quality Award, "to recognize U.S. companies that excel in quality achievement and quality management." We decided to interview Baldrige Award recipients for several reasons. First, since they all had experienced the same application and assessment process, we were able to compare different-sized companies from different industries. Second, since a national panel of experienced, impartial examiners and judges helped select the recipients, we had, in essence, a "quality control" mechanism to gauge their Quality efforts: these companies are successful, not only because we say so and they say so, but because outside quality experts say so, too. Finally, educators increasingly are using Baldrige-type Quality criteria as an organizational self-assessment tool, to track systemic improvement initiatives. Therefore, reporting practices of the Baldrige Award winners enhances the likelihood of business-education collaborations being formed around common organizational assessment issues.

We selected four of the Baldrige Award winners to interview, based on the information that would most likely be useful to educators. The companies we interviewed and the reasons are as follows.

Xerox. We *piloted* the project and conducted the most extensive interviews at the Xerox Corporation, for several reasons. To begin with, the transformation process using Quality was systemic, involving nearly the entire organization. Leadership focused primarily on changing the organizational culture to support teamwork, rather than on the statistical side of TQM. Top executives provided training to the entire corporation—to over 100,000 employees, including themselves. Xerox is well regarded for its benchmarking practices, which enable the company to improve continuously by learning from the best. And like public education, key company operations are unionized. Finally, we selected Xerox because many of its employees, beginning with former CEO and former U.S. Deputy Secretary of Education David Kearns, have actively engaged educators in applying Quality practices and tools in education.

Motorola. At Motorola, we conducted interviews that focused on *training* and *leadership* issues. We interviewed the staff of Motorola University on how a high-performance company evaluates the impact of its training on improving individual and organizational productivity. We also talked to company leaders about how Motorola applies *Six Sigma* (the effort to make error-free products and processes by eliminating defects and reducing cycle time) to all types of work processes and functions.

Globe Metallurgical. We purposely selected a *small-company* Baldrige winner (500 or fewer full-time employees) comparable in size to most school districts. We wanted to learn how a company with only fourteen people in its corporate headquarters and without a Quality staff infrastructure or substantial training resources tailors its products to meet diverse customer requirements.

Federal Express. We wanted to see if Quality was practiced any differently in a *service company,* which is likely to be more comparable to an education setting. Federal Express also is well known for three attributes that could benefit education: (1) a philosophy that celebrates its own employees (internal cus-

tomers) as the best way to satisfy external customers and be prof-
itable, (2) sophisticated use of technology in key aspects of its
work processes, and (3) a penchant for measuring and tracking
customer satisfaction indicators.

Education Sites

Appendix A contains demographic information on each education site as well as the name and address of the superintendent
or principal. Our selection of education sites followed a less
definitive process. The absence of a National Quality Award in
education meant that we could not rely on a common standard
of success and criteria, as we had done in choosing the companies. Therefore, we depended primarily on word of mouth,
based on two preconditions: (1) education sites that had the
longest experience with implementing Quality, particularly where
such efforts involved students, or (2) sites that represented a
range of settings and implementation models.

Although there is growing interest and discussion in education regarding TQM, much activity remains at the formative
stages. Therefore, the impact is generally less comprehensive
and less rooted than in business. In addition, many Quality initiatives in education are not systemic in nature—that is, they are
pioneered at the school rather than at the district level. Moreover, most advanced efforts to implement TQM in education
tend to be found in small, rural, or suburban settings rather
than in large systems, particularly large urban districts.

Collectively, the seven education sites in this study should
be viewed as a representative sample, rather than as the total
population of educators who are implementing TQM. The
seven sites are as follows.

Rappahannock County Public Schools, Virginia.   We chose
Rappahannock because it was one of eight school districts in
Virginia that was being trained by Xerox staff in using their
Quality methodology. Rappahannock gave us the opportunity
to assess the experiences of applying a *business training model*
directly to education.

Prince William County School District, Virginia.   Prince
William was also one of the "Xerox 8." We included it in our
sample because it is the *third largest school district* in Virginia and

because the superintendent is using TQM as the strategy to advance implementation of school-based management. Staff at three of the district's sixty-one schools have received training and are piloting the change effort.

Mt. Edgecumbe High School, Alaska. Individuals with only a passing familiarity with TQM are likely to recognize the name of Mt. Edgecumbe. It is the public residential high school in Alaska—made famous by PBS specials and numerous articles— that is using Deming's Quality Management philosophy and technology to transform the nature of *classroom instruction.* We visited Mt. Edgecumbe primarily to interview the students, many of whom come from family settings not unlike those in urban or poor rural communities but who have been trained to use Quality practices and tools successfully to assess their own learning progress.

Southwestern Wisconsin Quality Consortium. The South-western Wisconsin Consortium in the Madison-Beloit area was conceived when three neighboring superintendents who had attended graduate school together began to merge their interest in Deming's philosophy with outcome-based education. We selected the consortium for our study in order to capture how an *interdistrict collaborative* could serve as a potential role model for other districts, sharing financial resources on professional development as well as pooling staff expertise across the districts and integrating diverse management styles. We visited four of the six member districts—Beloit Turner, Brodhead, Oregon, and Parkview.

Vermont State Department of Education. We chose Vermont for the following reasons: The state has a strategic education plan, with specific goals, developed through a statewide collaborative effort. The Department of Education restructured recently in order to enhance cross-functional decision making. Department staff were trained by the National Center on Education and the Economy, using Xerox's Quality methodology. Education staff, in turn, trained their colleagues in the Department of Human Services so that together they can improve their decision-making processes affecting the same population base: students and their parents. Interviewing in Vermont also gave us the opportunity to explore ways to link *state and district* systemic change efforts.

George Westinghouse Vocational and Technical High School, Brooklyn, New York. The only urban site in our study, George Westinghouse Vocational and Technical High School (VTHS), is a large urban school that draws its 1,700 students from all of New York City. Seventy-five percent of the students are African-American and 22 percent are Hispanic. Less than 1 percent are Caucasian. The dropout rate was only 7.8 percent (which had declined even further to 5.3 percent by December 1992) compared to the districtwide rate of 17.2 percent. We selected Westinghouse to learn how Quality could become a useful change strategy in transforming *urban* schools and school systems.

Millcreek Township School District, Pennsylvania. For the last six years, the local chamber of commerce has networked local government, industry, and education leadership through the Erie Excellence Council. The council meets regularly on quality issues and recognizes efforts to implement TQM by designating recipients of Quality awards. Erie and Millcreek Township School District, a neighboring school district practicing TQM, gave us the opportunity to learn how *community involvement* and support can reinforce long-term change efforts in education.

Actually, when we say that NAB selected these eleven sites, that is only half the story. We asked them to invite us. Fortunately, all of them did. They were eager to share their experiences. By providing useful information to others, these sites hoped to reinforce their ranks. They also were eager for feedback on how they and the other sites were doing. Continuous improvement, after all, never stops.

A Note of Caution and an Expression of Hope

A few final comments are in order before we get started.

First, the note of caution. The information contained in this book is not meant to be a panacea for the problems that beset American education. First of all, Quality is a means to an end, not an end in itself. It is, by definition a *continuous improvement process,* which can be used by all types of organizations, but not before they have articulated their vision, mission, and priorities as well as what indicators they will use to assess progress. Second, suggesting TQM as a continuous improvement process *in education* is not meant to denigrate current restructuring efforts that are primarily school based. Quite the contrary, it is meant to strengthen them by adding a *systemic* focus, by offering a way for them to connect to their district administration—and vice versa.

Nor is our advice meant to be a "cookie cutter" for how educators, with business support, can implement TQM. Applying a list of ten, or fifteen, or even a hundred prescribed points will hardly guarantee a Quality education system, or a Quality company for that matter. At the same time, in our unique celebration of American individualism and self-invention, we should not ignore the experiences of others. They can often "jump start" our own learning curves. The challenge is to strike an appropriate balance—to benefit from but not expect to replicate the activities of worthy role models. Role models do not necessarily supply the right answers. But they can help others address the right questions.

And an expression of hope. As difficult as it will be to restructure education systems using Quality, it is worth the effort. Students who are educated in a Quality environment act differently. Trained to assess their own continuous progress, they also accept responsibility for becoming educated. They develop the will and the ability to become lifelong learners. The challenge for adults is to design an education system that engages students in this way.

Chapter 2

Defining Quality

Before we can explore further the potential of using Quality practices to transform education, it probably would be a good idea to define TQM. This chapter provides two definitions drawn from collaborative efforts between business and education sectors. The first comes from On Purpose Associates in Lansing, Michigan, a consulting firm that is working with a number of school districts to implement TQM: "Total Quality Management is a philosophy and set of principles that uses leadership, quantitative methods, systems thinking, and empowerment to continuously improve an organization's capacity to meet current and future customer needs."

The second definition comes from the Total Quality Leadership Steering Committee, a coalition of companies forged to encourage institutions of higher education to teach and practice TQM. The Committee's November 1992 report cautions that "Total Quality is not yet a monolithic, standardized set of concepts, even though a considerable area of agreement has been established." The report suggests the following basic definition:

> *Total Quality is a people-focused management system that aims at continual increase of customer satisfaction at continually lower real cost. Total Quality is a total system*

*approach (not a separate area or program), and an inte-
gral part of high-level strategy; it works horizontally across
functions and departments, involves all employees, top to
bottom, and extends backwards and forwards to include
the supply chain and the customer chain. Total Quality
stresses learning and adaptation to continual change as
keys to organizational success.*

*The foundation of Total Quality is philosophical: the
scientific method. Total Quality includes systems, methods, and tools. The systems permit change; the philosophy
stays the same. Total Quality is anchored in values that
stress the dignity of the individual and the power of community action.[1]*

It is easy to understand why a single concise definition of
Quality does not exist. TQM is not a simple subject.

Much has been written about and is readily available on
the key principles of TQM.[2] Our intent here is not to reiterate
this information, but rather to provide an overview of Quality in
practice. Therefore, the remainder of this chapter highlights
TQM from the perspective of business and education leaders we
visited: what they say Quality is and what they are doing to implement it. Based on our interviews and observations, the what's of
Quality in practice can be boiled down to *a commitment to three
C's: customers, culture, and capacity.*

Customers: Serving Those Inside and Outside the Organization

At the sites we visited, TQM begins and ends with "the customer."
Customers define quality. And they come in two generic vari-
eties, the external customer and the internal customer.

[1]Total Quality Forum, *A Report of the Total Quality Leadership Steering Committee
and Working Councils* (Cincinnati, Ohio: The Procter & Gamble Co., 1992),
pp. 1–8.
[2]Appendix B contains a brief resource list. Chapter Five provides detailed
examples, organized under the seven Baldrige Categories, of how educators
are applying Quality. The similarities to other education restructuring
efforts, such as school-based decision making and performance-based education, should be noted.

The External Customer

We did not have to ask the companies who their external customers were. The answer in the private sector is self-evident. Their customers include anyone who buys their products or services, thereby enabling them to stay in business and earn a profit. It is equally obvious why these companies focus so tenaciously on satisfying their customers. They enjoy staying in business and earning a profit. But the commitment to their customers extends beyond making money. These companies also focus on creating value for their customers that will, in turn, enhance their customers' productivity and well-being.

Defining the external customer is more challenging for school systems than for the private sector. Are the customers of education students? their parents? employees? taxpayers? colleges and universities? All of the above? The crowded field of potential contenders notwithstanding, educators in this study had no trouble identifying their most important customers. "The pay-off is when the results [of implementing Quality] affect kids," observes Rappahannock Superintendent David Gangel.

While the primary customers are their students, educators in this study agreed that students also have customers—most notably, their parents and future professors or employers. The ultimate challenge for educators is to offer a product—learning—that satisfies a heterogeneous set of customers whose requirements often are not explicit or aligned.

Examples: The External Customer

- Motorola executives set one fundamental objective: *Total Customer Satisfaction.* Achieving it became every employee's overriding responsibility.
- When Xerox executives first introduced *Leadership Through Quality,* they set three priorities: improve customer satisfaction, increase return on assets (ROA), and increase market share. "In retrospect, we should have focused primarily on customer satisfaction," observes former CEO David Kearns. "When all three goals were presented to Xerox employees, they saw it as mixed signals." Experience at Xerox demon-

strated that satisfying customers results in higher ROA and greater market share.

- As part of its customer satisfaction process, Rappahannock County School District routinely distributes a parent survey. Parents are asked to rate the importance of such topics as student courtesy, academic rigor, quality of transportation and cafeteria service, and communication. District administrators then create problem-solving teams to address parents' key concerns.
- "We don't sell anything but service," admits Federal Express CEO Frederick W. Smith, "and quality service is what our customers expect of us." Federal Express defines quality service as having a 100 percent satisfied customer at the end of each transaction. That says a lot for a company that contends with inclement weather, traffic jams, and occasional civil disorder to deliver packages on time and in good shape.
- Periodically, all Globe employees, from the shop floor on up, visit their customers in order to understand their needs. They observe firsthand how only two or three pounds of their product—iron-based metals—are used in making Ford and General Motors engine parts. As a result, says CEO Arden Sims, "Globe employees understand the importance of consistency." It is a responsibility they take seriously. Doing their share to keep the auto industry competitive, Globe employees believe, serves their ultimate customer: American society.
- Local employers were pleased with the work of George Westinghouse VTHS students, yet refused to hire any more students. The reason: their speech skills were practically unintelligible. School staff got together to discuss the problem and agree on a solution. The result: each student is required to take a one-semester course to develop better speaking skills. Employers now say their needs have been met.

The Internal Customer

Not all employees have external customers. A lot of the work that goes into the final product is performed by people never seen by the external customer. Thus, integral to TQM is the con-

cept of the internal customer. Educators and businesspeople in
this study defined the internal customer as the person next in
line within their organizations who receives the product or output of the work, with each subseqent person adding something
of value. Some of these organizations, such as Federal Express,
have adopted an explicit strategy stating that the best way to satisfy their external customers is first to address the needs of their
internal customers.

Examples: The Internal Customer

- "People who come to work for a company have a set of
  essential questions that must be answered," acknowledged
  Federal Express CEO Smith in 1990.[3] " 'What's in this for
  me, what do you expect of me, where do I go if I need some
  help, where do I go to get justice if I run across a problem
  involving my career, and if I do a good job, will I get ahead?'
  If you want people to be interested in customer service, to
  take an interest in the company's affairs and relate those
  issues back to their own well-being, you have to answer
  those fundamental questions through very visible, understandable policies, procedures, and programs."
- Once administrators at George Westinghouse VTHS decided to implement TQM, they began by asking the faculty
  to identify their priorities on what needed to change.
  Together, they drew up a list of 23 barriers. A Quality Steering Committee of volunteer faculty and students is knock-
  ing them off one at a time.
- Xerox provided Quality training to its entire workforce,
  over 100,000 employees. "You need to start with your internal customers," cautions Xerox training manager Dave
  Muxworthy, "because if you start on the outside, all you
  do is raise expectations you can't meet."

A Word About the Word "Customer"

Some educators may object to the term *customer* and may prefer
to come up with their own terminology. Generic names such as

[3]Nancy Karabatsos, *Absolutely, Positively Quality* (Milwaukee, Wis.: American
Society for Quality Control, 1990). (Manager's Pak reprint.)

recipient, beneficiary, and *client* or references to specific education stakeholders such as *student, parent, teacher, employer,* and so on can serve just as well. For consistency, however, we will use the term *customer.*

In implementing Quality, the challenge for all organizations is to analyze work as a series of transactions between suppliers (providers) and customers (recipients). Each transaction produces an output designed to meet or anticipate customer needs. As work proceeds, decisions are made, and individuals interact, the identity of the customer becomes situational. And it may flip back and forth. Students, for example, are the customers of their teacher's lesson plans. Teachers, in turn, are the customers of their students' homework assignments. Far from being an intellectual exercise, identifying and serving one's customers is critical to the successful functioning of any organization. Whether the term *customer* is used in education may be inconsequential. But whether the meaning behind the term is conveyed becomes absolutely essential.

Culture: Creating a Trusting Environment

Culture is something we saw and felt rather than captured verbally from our interviews. It relates to how people in organizations treat each other. The importance of a trusting culture in building a Quality environment cannot be overestimated. Its presence is absolutely essential. Employees must feel valued by their managers and supported by their colleagues before they can be motivated to contribute fully to improving their organizations.

Employees in Quality settings are made to feel that their actions matter to the overall success of their organization. Jobs are perceived not as stand-alone responsibilities, but rather as integral parts of a larger system, connected closely to what others contribute before and after. Trust needs to be built into decision-making processes so that employees, working together to address common problems, can craft acceptable, credible solutions. Trust must be earned and takes time to establish, especially in school systems where most teachers were prepared to work with groups of students but not collaboratively with adults.

Examples: The Culture

- A supportive culture predated Motorola's implementation of *Six Sigma,* its TQM initiative. Based on the company's origins in 1928 as a family business, succeeding generations of customers and employees have grown up together with Motorola, which values them equally. Quality has to become "personal," according to former CEO George Fisher, in order for it to come to life.
- Labor-management practices at Xerox already emphasized employee involvement. First championed by its union, the Amalgamated Clothing and Textile Workers, these positive working relationships evolved into employee empowerment under *Leadership Through Quality.* Both sides now share information during contract deliberations, which has enhanced mutual trust. TQM, according to union Vice President Tony Costanza, "teaches you how to justify solutions and test them. Negotiations have become less adversarial and are becoming a mutual problem-solving process."
- "If you want to succeed," observes Michael Graff, United Federation of Teachers Union Building representative, "you need to find ways that people can overcome obstacles, instead of just assuming that teachers will resist." The comraderie among administrators, teachers, and students at this Brooklyn-based high school thrives in sharp contrast to the metal detector and security guards stationed at the front door.
- David Gangel's low-key style masks a quiet intensity. The Rappahannock superintendent relates how he has to refrain from giving his staff the answers when facilitating problem-solving sessions. "Everyone has to change," concedes Gangel.
- Mt. Edgecumbe students are not hesitant to speak openly about their experiences with Quality. "This is not top down," asserts senior class president Omen Wild in a freewheeling session with his teachers and the superintendent. "If it were, it wouldn't work."

While we are on the subject of creating trusting environments, there probably is nothing more antithetical to establishing successful business-education relations than having business leaders refer to students as their "products." Granted, in true Quality-ese, students may well be the "output" of the relationship between schools as suppliers and employers as customers. Yet students are not inanimate objects or innocent bystanders. They are an important player in Quality education settings, as both the primary customer and as front-line workers. Consequently, students need to have a say in and accept responsibility for their own learning processes. Viewed from this perspective, the "product" of the most important relationship in education—the one between students and teachers—is "learning." And the "profit" is gains in student achievement.

Capacity: Designing a System for Continuous Improvement

The companies we visited have been practicing TQM for a number of years. They are customer focused. Their cultures are grounded in a sense of trust. Employees are using Quality tools to improve their work processes and track results. Now these companies are taking Quality to the next steps. Their leaders are seeking ways to manage and sustain the change process itself. Throughout their organizations, they are attempting to assess the impact of their initial successes and the need for subsequent action. They are trying to design into their work processes a "constancy of purpose," as Deming would say, that will sustain improvement efforts even when key individuals turn over. Seen in this light, Quality is more than one person's charisma. It becomes the organization's charisma, the way the entire company "does business" all the time. Successful companies, in other words, institutionalize organizational capacity to be able to make continuous improvements.

How do organizations reach this point? High-performance organizations generally have found that flattening their hierarchies, blurring the boundaries between functional units, and operating in cross-functional teams is a key business advantage. Effective teams position organizations to solve problems, address priorities, and identify business opportunities more quickly. For these improvements to occur, however, employees often need training to acquire new skills. They also must be afforded the opportunity, support, and resources to exercise such skills. Quality organizations recognize and reinforce desired behaviors through the ways they are structured and provide incentives to their employees.

Examples: The Capacity for Continuous Improvement

- Federal Express, several years into its Quality efforts, created an Office of Internal Audits and Quality Assurance, reporting to the CEO. The purpose is to oversee, coordinate, and reinforce the company's TQM initiatives, which are the responsibility of the individual business units. "People have to be able to understand how you go about managing quality in a common manner," explains Fred Smith. "It has to cut across all organizational lines."
- Xerox now has a common business language worldwide. Training all employees to use the same Quality tools guarantees their immediate participation in solving problems no matter the office or the country. "Once you've changed the structure so that everyone is doing it," notes Customer Services Manager Susie Fenwick, "it's hard to go back because then you'd be fighting the system."
- Executives of Motorola University have challenged themselves to determine the true value-added of training. They are trying to craft a way to measure the direct impact of employee training not only on individual performance but, ultimately, on organizational productivity. Motorola wants to create a "learning organization," says Debby King, head of senior executive training programs.
- Following leadership transitions, both Xerox and Motorola were able to validate their success in institutionalizing Quality practices. When the original Quality champions left or assumed different roles, the change efforts they had launched not only survived but continued to flourish under their successors.

The reader will note that the previous examples are all from the companies. This is no accident. In contrast to business, implementing Quality in education is relatively new. Most educators are concerned primarily with obtaining the appropriate training for their employees and defining, let alone improving, their work processes. Building internal capacity to make continuous improvements remains a not-so-distant but future challenge in education.

If their experiences are similar to those in business, however, inevitably education leaders will need to create a system where the whole is greater than the sum of its parts. In essence, educators will need to redesign their organizations so that the work of everyone inside schools, and of those working to support schools, centers on the thirteen- to fourteen-year learning cycle of each child in becoming a lifelong learner.

Chapter 3

Getting Down to Cases
Business and Education

Chapter Three contains profiles of two companies we visited, Xerox and Federal Express, and one school district, Millcreek Township. The purpose of highlighting these as case studies is not to focus on the sites as ends in themselves (which is why we did not present all eleven sites) but rather as examples of how complex organizations undergo comprehensive change over time. The three cases are intended to be illustrative rather than all-inclusive. They underscore the reality that although the principles of Quality may be consistent across organizations, the strategies and experiences of organizations in implementing TQM are likely to differ.

Quality at Xerox: Creating a Revolution from Within

In 1959, Xerox invented an industry when it introduced the world's first plain paper copier. During the 1960s, business soared as increasing numbers of companies discovered that they could not live without a copier. But by the mid 1970s, Xerox had to face the loss of its exclusive patent and aggressive competition at home and abroad. By 1982, Xerox had lost 50 percent of the market, and the future did not look any brighter. Its Japanese competitors were selling low-end copiers for what it cost

Xerox to manufacture them. And these same companies were developing new products twice as fast.

How bad was the news? Pretty bad, according to David Kearns's own account of when he became CEO in 1982. "To put it bluntly," writes Kearns, "if nothing were done to correct things, we were destined to have a fire sale and close down by 1990. And the final humiliation for me was that it would be on my watch. This could be my legacy: I had put the company out of business."[1] "Fortunately, Xerox reacted in time," notes current CEO Paul Allaire. "In the early 80s, we got serious about Quality and used it to turn the company around. We involved our entire workforce in becoming part of the solution."

Transforming Xerox

As CEO in 1982, Kearns knew that he had to take action. In analyzing the successful results of Fuji/Xerox, he observed that their Japanese partner did business differently. And it showed in the results. Where Xerox was in danger of going under, profits at Fuji/Xerox had increased 20 percent in one year. On return visits to Japan, Kearns brought his senior managers and the company's union leader with him so they could study operations at Fuji/Xerox. Meanwhile, Xerox executives also were consulting with the Quality gurus stateside. They talked with experts such as W. Edwards Deming and Joseph Juran and participated in Philip Crosby's Quality training. Ultimately, however, Xerox used what it had learned from these "outside experts" and turned to the "inside experts"—its own people—to invent its change process. "We needed to use our own terminology and apply Quality tools to the real work that people are doing," recalls Kearns. "We needed to convince our people internally to buy into the changes."

At a management retreat in 1983, the top twenty-five senior executives signed off on the effort to craft a business plan to implement Quality at Xerox. They selected fifteen key staff from across the company to form a Quality implementation

---

[1]David T. Kearns and David A. Nadler, *Prophets in the Dark* (New York: HarperBusiness, 1992), p. xiv.

team. Their task: write a five-year plan, which became known inside Xerox as the Green Book. Working closely with organization development consultant David Nadler, over the next few months team members developed *Leadership Through Quality*, their Quality strategy. The team built on successful existing practices in which Xerox employees at all levels were invested: the commitment of senior executives to competitive benchmarking, of middle managers to developing interactive skills, and of union and line workers to active employee involvement in decision making.

The Green Book included five-year goals with annual targets: increase profits (return on assets), increase market share, and improve customer satisfaction. The plan represented a long-term implementation strategy to redesign key work processes at Xerox and ultimately to transform the Xerox culture. The collection of disparate superstars that had invented an industry would now become *Team Xerox*, team players in pursuit of a common goal—quality in meeting the needs of external and internal customers.

Quality Training: Changing Management Behavior

A key element of the Xerox change strategy was training that would change the organization's behavior, above all the individualistic management style of its leaders. If the company expected employees at all levels to make decisions collaboratively, it had to give them new problem-solving tools and reinforce interpersonal and team-building skills. In essence, the company had to develop a common language for making decisions. Consequently, Xerox developed its own Quality curriculum. From 1984 through 1988, all 100,000 employees received the same forty hours (later reduced to twenty-eight hours) of Quality training. Starting with Kearns and the senior vice presidents, the training cascaded like a waterfall down the entire organization. Everyone except the CEO and the people with no direct reports received two exposures to the training—first they learned *Leadership Through Quality* from their managers, then they taught it to their employees. Training took place in family groups so that employees would use the new tools and skills on real work and real priorities. This training strategy reinforced implementation. "Even if you didn't believe in it at the time," recalled former Xerox manager Norm Deets, "you had to understand it well enough to be able to train your own employees."

Putting Quality into Operation

Xerox created a Quality infrastructure to manage the change process. Trainers were assigned to each of the operating units and facilitated their use of the Quality tools. Later, Xerox added statistical tools to the general training and developed customized training to meet the needs of specific audiences: managers, accountable for overseeing the progress of their employees and suppliers, accountable to Xerox for delivering Quality products. Senior executives also built support for Quality decision making into key work processes. Managers are rated on their use of Quality tools and their effectiveness as supportive bosses counts in decisions regarding their promotions. Assigning up-and-coming line managers as Quality staff for several years before their promotion to senior executive positions underscores the importance that Xerox places on implementing *Leadership Through Quality*. Instilling an appreciation for Quality among Xerox's future senior executives also reinforces the likelihood of its long-term practice.

Initiating a self-assessment process in 1987 based on the Baldrige Award Criteria enabled Xerox executives to identify what they called an additional 500 "warts" that needed attention. Preparing the company's Baldrige Award application for consideration in 1989 became a way for Xerox to codify and track its improvement activities. Winning the Baldrige Award supplied a surge of momentum to the long-term improvement effort. Addressing these problem areas, as well as using feedback from frequent customer surveys, formed the bedrock over the next five years of Xerox's continuous improvement plan.

Xerox also reinforces organizational commitment to Quality by celebrating and disseminating experiences across the entire corporation. Each year, the company showcases successful teams in a companywide TeamWork Day simulcast to the largest offices across the country. In 1989, CEO Paul Allaire instituted Presidential Reviews, conducted quarterly, which are internal assessments of new products and key functions that are company priorities. In a meeting before the top executives, senior managers present studies conducted by cross-functional teams using Quality tools. The reviews analyze what worked and what did not, in order to communicate and replicate successful practices companywide.

Results

For three years, Kearns refused to allow the results of *Leadership Through Quality* to be measured. He understood that behavioral changes take time and that measuring results prematurely could jeopardize the change effort. "First, we had to learn to inspect our processes," notes Kearns, "not just our outcomes."

By 1989, however, "The Document Company" (as Xerox refers to itself) could document impressive results. Xerox became the first U.S. company to win back market share from the Japanese without government supports. The same year, Xerox won the Baldrige Award. By 1990, return on assets had increased to 14.6 percent from 7.8 percent in 1986. Corporate income had increased to $599 million from $314 million. The percentage of defect-free parts in Xerox copiers had improved to 99.96 percent from 92 percent. Xerox had reduced both its manufacturing costs and its product development cycle time by 50 percent. In September 1990, the company implemented its Total Satisfaction Guarantee policy: hereafter, any Xerox equipment acquired by a customer would either be fixed or replaced at the customer's discretion over the next three years for any reason short of being destroyed by an Act of God.

A subsequent reorganization in 1992 was designed to increase the corporation's competitive edge. In an effort to respond more quickly to the market, CEO Allaire decentralized the manufacturing operations into nine autonomous business units. Each unit remains linked strategically through the use of technology and customer-focused operating divisions. "The moves are being made to enable Xerox to provide faster response time to customers and markets, to push responsibility and accountability further down the organization, and to permit

Figure 3.1. Xerox: A Quality Revolution.

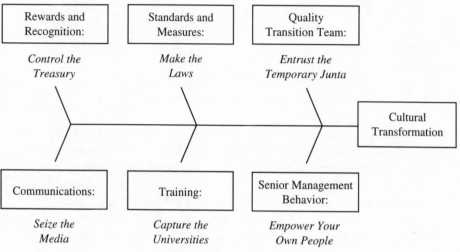

Source: Generated by Xerox Corporation staff.

employees to exercise greater entrepreneurial skills," according to Allaire in a news release announcing the reorganization.

In Retrospect

During the late 1980s, Xerox did not come close to meeting the goals outlined in its initial five-year plan. But it did not matter, according to Xerox officials, because the change effort enabled the company to set a new direction. Today, Xerox is recognized nationally as one of the early and most thorough corporate leaders of America's Quality Movement. But it took nearly a decade to achieve this distinction. Improvement efforts, as noted above, continue.

Reflecting on the change process at Xerox during the 1980s, Executive Vice President Wayland Hicks recalls: "At first there was a lot of skepticism and cynicism because TQM came from Japan. And it was viewed as the latest flavor of the month. But David [Kearns] was high energy. People liked him a lot and wanted to support him. He was active and visible and not just talk." Seeing the possibilities in Japan forged Kearns's commitment to implementing Quality at Xerox. But it did not provide him with the answers on how Xerox should do it. In developing the how's, Kearns turned to his own employees. And in the process of transforming their culture, depicted in Figure 3.1, Xerox employees created a Quality revolution from within.

Quality at Federal Express:
Enhancing the Corporate Philosophy

Federal Express, like Xerox, invented an industry. Overnight air express was born on April 17, 1973, with a fleet of seven aircraft and delivery of eight packages, seven of them sent as trial runs to other FedEx employees. Since then, the Memphis-based company has grown to over 96,000 full-time equivalent (FTE) employees and transports an average of nearly two million packages nightly, using a fleet of 30,000 vehicles operating in 187 countries.

Unlike Xerox (and most companies), however, Federal Express was founded on Quality practices. "What set us apart from the very earliest days," says founder and CEO Fred Smith, "was an absolutely zealous approach to quality and customer satisfaction." *People-Service-Profit* (or *P-S-P*) has been the guiding corporate philosophy since 1973. "When people are placed first, they will provide the highest possible service, and profits will follow," explains Smith.

What drew Federal Express to TQM was not a fear of going out of business. Quite the opposite. Phenomenal growth and functional diversity have been the company's hallmark. Guaranteeing 100 percent customer satisfaction—in the face of such growth and diversity—has been the company's greatest challenge. Product is not defined in the typical sense at Federal Express. The company sells speed and reliability. It commits to delivering the products of its customers on time and damage free. To fulfill this commitment, however, senior executives need constant feedback from their customers, internal as well as external.

Gravitating to TQM

As Federal Express grew, so did the number and cost of its customer complaints. Increasing volume meant that the company could no longer rely on percentages to satisfy its customers. For a company that was delivering over a million packages a day, a 99 percent customer approval rating still meant more than 10,000 irate customers.

Most dissatisfied customers simply take their business elsewhere. When they do, they tend to share their displeasure—not with the company but with other people, which multiplies the potential business loss. To prevent such defections, Federal Express needed a way to anticipate and preempt customer complaints. According to Tom Oliver, former executive vice president: "We knew that we had to reduce costs and improve quality. We also knew, based on customer complaints and feedback from our sales force, that we did not have an effective strategy to do it."

Initial Efforts

Federal Express first became interested in TQM during the early 1980s, when its various business divisions began looking at quality programs modeled on the principles of Crosby, Deming, and Juran. By the mid 1980s, the company began to consolidate its efforts.

Company employees frequently cite a favorite Smith saying: "If you can't measure it, you can't manage it." For a company that lives by the numbers—volume of packages, arrival and departure times—it was natural that Federal Express would look first to the "hard side" of Quality. Federal Express managers describe their initial foray into TQM, charitably, as a "false start." In 1984, the senior executives sequestered themselves for a week to learn about statistical process control. The response was less than gratifying. "If I have to be a statistician to do Quality," vowed one senior vice president, "I won't do it!" The quantitative approach turned everyone off.

So the Quality advocates in-house pursued a different strategy, more in tune with a corporate culture that celebrates its own people. What began as a top-down effort now switched to bottom-up. A Quality Action Team calling itself the "skunk works group," according to former Quality Improvement Manager John West, "went underground." After working for two years with consultants Organizational Dynamics Inc. (ODI) to develop the "soft side" of TQM, the team felt that it could demonstrate success. Next, team members actively pursued the backing of some patron saints. In 1987, they prepared a presentation illustrating how Quality practices could save the company money for the three senior vice presidents most likely to be supportive. The senior executives "bought off on it," according to West, and began to implement quality programs in their divisions. By 1988, several efforts were in full swing. Their success inspired the other divisions to buy in, too.

Quality Training

Providing Quality training is the responsibility of each business division at Federal Express. However, the company is training everyone uniformly on quality structures and processes, developed with their consultants. The structure is empowered Quality Action Teams or QATs. FADE, short for Focus-Analyze-Develop-Execute, is the four-step problem-solving process used by each QAT. (A visitor to Federal Express quickly notices two things: the enormity of the main Hub, which sorts the packages each night, and the widespread use of acronyms. Nearly everything is known by its initials.) Staff also are trained on the typical Quality processes and tools, such as engaging in brainstorming sessions and using fishbone diagrams, pareto charts, and so on. In addition, Federal Express trains its employees to use Customer-Supplier Alignments (an apparent exception to the acronym rule) that facilitates decisions between two parties when a QAT is not needed. The supplier asks the customer three key questions: (1) What do you need from me? (2) What do you do with what I give you? and (3) What are the gaps between (1) and (2)?

Other Elements That Complement Their Quality Efforts

When Federal Express won the Baldrige Award, examiners commended the company on the strength of its "people-first" policies and programs. TQM took hold at Federal Express because of these programs, which undergird the company's focus on meeting customer needs, both inside and outside the company. They include the following.

- *Service Quality Indicators* (*SQI*) are quantitative indicators that enable employees daily to track how well they are serving their customers. The twelve indicators are weighted according to the severity of the problem from the customer's perspective—lost or damaged packages and missed pickups being the most cardinal of the customer-related sins.
- *Customer Satisfaction Index* (*CSI*) is qualitative customer information, obtained from a quarterly survey of 2,100 Federal Express customers, selected randomly. Participants are asked to articulate their service satisfaction using a five-point scale on fifty questions. The results are then aggregated and reviewed by senior managers.

The SQI and CSI are the primary means by which Federal Express addresses the "S" in People-Service-Profit. The "People" part is addressed through a number of programs, which are too numerous to mention here.[2] However, the key mechanism is the SFA:

- The *Survey-Feedback-Action* (*SFA*) is a bottom-up performance review, completed anonymously each year by all employees, which serves as a report card for their respective managers. Responses assess not only a manager's performance from the employees' perspective, but also the performance of the manager's boss. The results, which are tabulated electronically, are used in group feedback sessions. Each unit is then responsible for formulating a Quality action plan to address problem areas. Federal Express also aggregates the results so that senior executives can identify and track over time the company's management training needs, which are then addressed through its Leadership Institute.
    Performance reviews travel top down as well. It is the responsibility of each manager, from the highest levels of

---

[2]For a more inclusive review of these programs, see Federal Express, *Information Book* (Memphis, Tenn.: Federal Express, n.d.), and the American Management Association, *Blueprints for Service Quality: The Federal Express Approach* (New York: American Management Association, 1991).

the company down through the ranks, to conduct six-month performance reviews.

Because Federal Express has developed these and other indicators to assess company and employee performance, the quality tools and processes are grounded in a strong organizational context. They have been summarized here to make an important point: TQM has become the business strategy through which the company achieves its corporate goals. Federal Express also puts its money where its mouth is, literally. Executives are rewarded on the basis of company performance on the P-S-P indicators. Failure to meet objectives in all three categories means no annual bonuses. And the company is serious: 1990, the year the company received the Baldrige Award, was the same year that executives went without bonuses.

Impact of the Baldrige Award

Winning the Baldrige Award in 1990 may have taken Federal Express by surprise (according to numerous interviews), but it energized the company's Quality efforts. Executives felt that the company had to live up to its reputation. "Opening our kimonos to show the world how we 'did Quality,'" recalls Quality Manager Jean Ward Jones, "helped us realize how much more still needed to be done." The fact that Federal Express won was "nice," according to the CEO Fred Smith, but the real reward was in what they learned about their own company. Smith refers to the award as "their license to practice."

Recent Efforts

Responsibility for implementing TQM rests with each division, where Quality staff report to line managers. In the effort to reinforce its continuous improvement efforts companywide, Federal Express has integrated its Quality and self-assessment functions within the Office of Internal Audit and Quality Assurance. The office works with the Quality staff assigned to the divisions, who are networked through a Quality Advisory Board. The office also serves the Executive Quality Board which networks senior executives from each division so that Federal Express can oversee its Quality efforts companywide. The challenge is to "direct quality" so that the entire organization can achieve its never-ending goal of continuous improvement.

Results

Federal Express continues to grow and change its business. The company takes risks and has made some false steps along the way. Consequently, the bottom line in recent years no longer mirrors the go-go 1970s and early 1980s, when 20 percent annual profits were not uncommon.

Company executives feel that implementing Quality has helped Federal Express improve where it counts, however—with its P-S-P indicators. The year it instituted its formal Quality processes, employees taking the SFA gave the company the highest leadership scores in over ten years. And in 1989, the number of quantifiable customer-related mistakes (the Service Quality Indicators) went down, despite a 20 percent increase in package volume.

Favorable results show up in behaviors as well as the numbers. They can "drive out fear"—a good thing, as Deming would say. For example, not killing the messenger is both formal and informal company policy at Federal Express. Jerry Leary, managing director of the Capital district (Washington, D.C.), describes how he initiated a "risk-takers award" to recognize Quality Action Teams that completely "belly-flopped." "Employees may have a good idea on its face and try hard," explains Leary, "but it just may not pan out." The practice enables employees to make light of such escapades. But it also makes good business sense. Risk taking often is necessary before an organization can solve its problems or make quantum-leap discoveries. It also enhances productivity since others, once informed, are less inclined to repeat the same mistakes than if they always have to fly solo. Risk taking can occur on an individual scale as well. Jeanne Hearn, an executive assistant in sales and customer service, explains how she would rather do something and make a mistake than sit back and do nothing. The reason? The customer—her boss—has empowered her to try.

In Retrospect

When asked if he would have done anything differently in introducing TQM to Federal Express, Smith responds: "There was too much emphasis on the tools too early, rather than educating people on why you want quality to begin with. Quality is more cultural. The tools should become a means to an end, rather than an end in themselves." Employees told us that Smith's allegiance to implementing TQM never wavered, despite the company's initial wrong turn with a statistical approach. And they credit their CEO's persistence with getting the rest of the senior managers on board. Employees also emphasize the need for success stories early on, which give people the necessary direction and encouragement.

Jack Finley, former vice president for aircraft maintenance at Federal Express, sums up his experience with Quality this way: "We had to learn the hard way that the people who produce for you know a helluva lot more than you do. [TQM] doesn't take away management's prerogatives. We still need to make decisions. But letting your employees do their jobs and having them tell you how to do yours is a 'win-win.' Even if it doesn't work all the time, it gets everyone working together."

Millcreek Township School District: Pollinating Quality

Millcreek's Quality saga is not one of redeeming a floundering school district with consistently low test scores or financial troubles. Instead, by most people's definitions, Millcreek has done a fine job of educating its children. With 7,500 students in twelve schools, Millcreek serves the contiguous western and southern area surrounding the city of Erie. The district has a history of achieving students, community partnerships, and lengthy tenured administrators and teachers. Verel Salmon, Millcreek assistant superintendent since 1982, puts it this way: "Millcreek had a focus on excellence which was like Quality. We never got to the point of crisis. We just always tried to do better." Salmon, who has been with the district since 1978, is Millcreek's acknowledged Quality champion.

Millcreek's Culture

Millcreek's culture is one of trust and motivated employees, teachers and nonteachers alike. Far from existing in isolation, the school district sees its surrounding community as its customers. In fact, Millcreek has been using TQM-like practices since the 1970s. The district formed a Customer Advisory Council in 1978 to involve the community in its schools and a districtwide faculty Quality Enhancement Committee in 1985 to improve the quality of instruction.

Even so, by the mid 1980s the community of Millcreek had realized that if they were to maintain their reputation of excellence, they had to find even more successful ways to conduct "the business of teaching students." Encouraged by their TQM-like activities, the school district began its official study of TQM in 1986, the same year William DeCrease, then a Quality program manager for the Lord Corporation, established the Erie Excellence Council (EEC) to bring TQM to Erie.

Erie Excellence Council

The Erie Excellence Council, a division of the Erie Area Chamber of Commerce, established committees covering various elements of community life in Erie (industry, education, health, and so on) to improve their functions in the community. The committees meet monthly to use Quality principles and tools to focus their improvement efforts. The committees measure progress against a Vision for 1999 on an annual basis. The Academic Committee, with Millcreek Assistant Superintendent Salmon as its head, has been an EEC stalwart from the beginning. It has also been an important variable in the success of Millcreek Township's continuous improvement vision and goal. Prior to establishing its Vision for 1999, the Academic Committee developed a "Community Quality Curriculum," based on the committee members' notions of what education should look like in the community by 1999. They also met with the Industrial Committee to assess workplace skill requirements and the subsequent necessary education changes.

Using Quality problem-solving and process tools, the Academic Committee came up with sixty-three descriptors, categorized them together with the input from the EEC Industrial Committee, and listed twelve categories of academic issues: Quality, Choice, Meeting Customer (Employer) Needs, Global Perspective, Values, Community Service by Students, The Basic Curriculum, Community Support, Competencies, Administration and Organization, Reducing Wasted Student Opportunity, and Colleges and Teacher Preparation. Academic subcommittees elaborated and refined the vision in each of the twelve areas. The subcommittees spent the 1991–92 school year developing Action Plans, and efforts are currently directed to implementing the vision across northwestern Pennsylvania.

Millcreek's Quality Moves

At the same time that the EEC Quality mission was establishing its priorities, the Millcreek Township School District was involved in its own Quality initiatives. Millcreek encouraged staff members throughout the district to enroll in local companies' Quality training courses and to visit other districts that were changing their education processes. Simultaneously, with support from futurist Joel Barker, the school district developed a Vision Statement, which serves as a reference tool for continuous improvement. The theme in Millcreek is transformation. It is inclusive and fosters activity at all levels—among support staff, administrators, teachers, and students. Millcreek has purposely refrained from introducing Quality activities sequentially. Instead of a formal cascading of training for all staff, it has encouraged Quality activities to "take off." As a result, many teams and projects have been initiated simultaneously—almost like spontaneous combustion—as staff attend different training sessions and meetings and talk and plan among themselves.

Robert Agnew, superintendent in Millcreek since 1981 and an educator for forty years, is excited about the potential of TQM in his school district. "It translates into recognizing the talents of people and empowering them to use those talents to make decisions that will bring about continuous improvement for the school district and, ultimately, the students," he says. "We're not just practicing the same things over and over. That's what continuous improvement is about. It's how we're going to keep getting better and better." He also acknowledges that Salmon's insistence and persistence have kept the efforts in Millcreek growing and exciting.

The Many Benefits of Problem-Solving Teams

As part of the district's formal TQM study, Millcreek hired TAI, a consultant group specializing in TQM training, to assist it in addressing some of its barriers to improvement. The first TAI group addressed problems with the district's food service operation, which was losing $50,000 per year. A group of two administrators, two food service managers, and a food service supervisor attended the training together and then began their problem-solving activities. They broke even after their year-long team activity. Millcreek assigned other teams to improve instruction (for example, the "Mathletes") and custodial services; additional teams have been trained internally.

Jay Musarra is an assistant principal at the McDowell Intermediate (grades nine and ten) High School. He participated in the first TAI training group on food service and he is a member of the EEC. He is also a member of the district's Quality Advisory Committee, a group of five administrators who work with Verel Salmon to foster Total Quality techniques throughout Millcreek. Musarra credits his TQM training and applications for changing his approach to problem solving. "I have learned to set a goal and get to the end results," he says. He also has praise for his involvement with the EEC. "I feel as though I am much more able to get the community leaders' attention, and I benefit from studying what others are doing. Plus, I feel much less isolated from the community." Musarra sees many advantages to using TQM, not the least of which is the district's current emphasis on improving teachers' skills and abilities. "Ultimately, with our focus on cooperative learning and working, we are teaching each other how to teach better. It all comes together."

Planning a New School Building

In 1988, a planning team comprised of administrators, teachers, parents, nonteaching staff, and other community members began meeting with an outside facilities planner to talk about the way they wanted a new Belle Valley School to look and to work. Two years later, Belle Valley has received nationwide acclaim as a School of the Future. It is outfitted with over 400 Macintosh computers—in classrooms, in the library, and in the administrative offices—to ensure that technology is fully integrated into all of the students' learning processes. The school, which is quintessentially student focused, reflects the thoughtful considerations that were made by those who best know schools and the customers they serve. The school won the Council of Educational Facility Planners International (CEFPI) prestigious MacConnell Award for planning processes. (For more about the Belle Valley School, see Chapter Five.)

The same planning process, used a second time around for the district's new middle school, took only seven months. The theme of this new middle school is "Community and World at Work." And in keeping with Millcreek's goal of providing its students with Quality experiences, the school will operate a series of student-run companies, as do the district's other middle and high schools.

Teams Throughout the District

Working with Assistant Superintendent Salmon, a team of six secretaries from the district's central office surveyed all district secretaries for their most tedious problem. They identified the travel request form and nine associated forms as the most frequently used and most objectionable form in the district. They decided to reduce the form by 50 percent. The team worked for a year, often on their own time. In 1992, they won one of the highest awards given in the Erie Excellence Council's 1992 Quality Award competition. When word of the "Form Cutters" got out, the maintenance staff asked for their assistance in trying to do some Quality problem solving. In 1992, secretaries from each school formed a team to tackle and reform their major aggravation: supply ordering and distribution. In addition, every building has developed a safety team, as has the district overall.

Winning the Erie Excellence Award

When the Millcreek Township School District applied for the Erie Excellence Council's 1992 Quality Award, it was their third time out. This time, however, district staff benchmarked against the previous winners to improve their processes throughout 1992. Regardless of having to compete against manufacturing and technical companies throughout the Erie area, they were determined to win. And they did.

Improved Student Learning—What It Is All About

The ultimate goal, of course, is to provide students with tools that will enable them to take charge of their own learning. Millcreek's use of the "company in the schools" concept teaches the principles of Total Quality and provides the students and their teachers opportunities to apply them. Initiated in 1982 as a way to integrate instruction from seemingly disparate subjects and classes, the companies have applied TQM since 1989. There are examples of this company concept throughout the district. The McDowell Clock Company, which designs, produces, and sells clocks out of the McDowell Intermediate High School, is the largest of a dozen student companies currently in operation. The economics teachers collaborated with a technology teacher; with their students and guidance from AMSCO, a district industrial partner, they formed the company. Students have learned about all aspects of forming a company that produces clocks as part of their economics class, and they use computer CAD/CAM and CNC machines to mass-produce a line of clocks for retail sale. Now a known entity in the community, the company is facing the issues associated with demand being greater than supply.

Elementary staff and students have utilized their partnership with Marine Bank to create working thrift banks in the schools. "In our middle schools," says Dennis Libra, assistant

principal at the Westlake Middle School and another member
of the Quality Advisory Committee, "students operate several
companies, including two desktop publishing companies, a
recycling company, a video production company, and a tropical
candy company that buys acreage in South American rain
forests with their revenue." Students at McDowell Senior High
School have constructed and now operate a campus store in
their main school lobby, which is also open to the public.

In Summary

Millcreek has implemented Total Quality Management techniques in many ways, including, but not limited to:

- Customer satisfaction surveys of regional employers
- A continuous improvement suggestion system
- The school board's quality policy and graduation require-
  ment that all students study Quality management
- The systematic integration of computer technology as a
  quality or productivity improvement tool
- Faculty-initiated instructional improvement groups meeting
  on their own time
- The "Form Cutters'" success in reducing ten time-
  consuming travel request and related forms to a user-
  friendly one-page, two-sided form
- Use of presidential audits

Explains Superintendent Agnew: "[Quality] is not another short-term educational fad. It's a long-term model for transforming the American education system."

Applying Millcreek's Experiences

Is Millcreek too idyllic a community from which to draw gener-
alizations about the application of TQM to education? Verel
Salmon admits that they benefit enormously by being in a community that values Quality, but speculates that they would be on
this same journey without the Erie Excellence Council. It may
have taken longer to get it started, and it may have taken a dif-

ferent course, but the spirit of continuous improvement can be fostered anywhere.

Their style of "100 flowers blooming" works for them because of the long-standing relationships of trust that exist in the district. "Nonetheless," says Salmon, "Millcreek is middle America. If Total Quality Management, as customized in Millcreek by its staff and students, can have such a powerful transformational effect here, then the same can happen in any school system across our great land."

Chapter 4

Implementation Strategies

Chapter Four showcases the dynamics of the change process itself. All too often, the recapping of "lessons learned" shares the *contents* of successful change efforts without articulating *how* the changes occurred. That is like expecting someone to design a house simply by giving the person a tour of your house. If the objective is to learn from other peoples' experiences, the how's—the blueprints, bricks, and mortar—need to accompany the what's.

Much insight can be gained from analyzing the implementation of Quality at different stages and in different settings. This chapter draws on the experiences of all eleven sites but focuses primarily on the four companies, since the next chapter is devoted exclusively to education. The information is organized according to critical decision points, aggregated under four implementation themes that track the change process. The four implementation themes are:

- Confronting early issues
- Moving from outside to inside
- Providing new tools
- Staying the course

Confronting Early Issues

We identified several key decision points in the early stages of the change process. First, each site had to have a critical and acknowledged reason to change. Second, each organization had a champion(s) with the courage to suggest a new way of doing business. Third, their leaders committed body and soul to the change effort and made it happen.

Recognizing the Need to Change

People do not get up one day and say, "Gee, I think it's time to transform my organization." To initiate the types of changes described here, the motivation has to be substantial. In the case of three of the four companies we studied—Globe, Motorola, and Xerox—the motivation was as substantial as it gets: *survival.* They realized that if they chose not to change, they might not be around in the future. We also saw evidence—in more subtle yet fundamental ways—of survival issues motivating the education sites. Survival, however, relates not to schools, but to children and communities. At George Westinghouse VTHS, we observed a class of eleventh graders calmly discussing whether students should be allowed to carry weapons, given the dangers they face in getting from home to school and back. Knowing that their "customers" are confronting such life-threatening choices is as great a motivator for educators like Principal Lewis Rappaport and Assistant Principal Franklin Schargel as it is for CEOs facing the potential demise of their company.

Implementing Quality need not be just about survival, however. The experience at Federal Express illustrates that some companies are motivated to *do what they do well, only better.* These companies already are focused on customers' needs. They simply want to create an organization that enables them to stay close to their customers, as those needs change. We found similar motivation at a number of our education sites. For example, many students from Vermont, Millcreek Township, and the Wisconsin Consortium do quite well on standard performance indicators when compared to other states or school districts. Many students do well, but not all students. Existing performance standards are used but are not world-class standards. Having committed themselves to helping *all* kids meet *higher* standards, educators from these same sites also concluded that standard operating procedures in education prevented them from delivering on that promise. And existing ways of doing business hampered them from focusing on future student needs.

Igniting Change: The Critical Role of the Champion

Someone has to be the spark plug of change: the instigator who not only sees the need for change but has an inkling of what to do about it. Motorola's foray into Quality began in 1979 with "The Big Bang," according to former CEO Robert Galvin. It happened the day one of his senior executives shocked the entire company into action by proclaiming before an international gathering of Motorola officers: "We aren't talking about the most important subject: quality. And our quality stinks!"

Champions also can take the form of a skunk works group at Federal Express that went underground or of the three senior executives who, having proved to their own satisfaction that implementing TQM made good business sense, "lateraled" it to the rest of their colleagues. The same phenomenon characterizes all seven education sites we visited. Whether it was a teacher at Mt. Edgecumbe, an assistant principal at George Westinghouse VTHS, an assistant superintendent at Millcreek, superintendents in Virginia and Wisconsin, or a staff team in the Vermont Department of Education—ultimately, all these "TQM champions" had the courage of their own convictions to suggest something new and the credibility inside their own organizations to be taken seriously.

Blessing, Committing to, Driving, Modeling, Implementing, and Reinforcing Change: The Essential Role of the Leader

Leaders can be the initial TQM champions, but they need not be. New ideas do not have to start with the leader, but eventually they must wind up there. Leaders, according to Xerox's

John Kelsch, have to play three roles for Quality implementation to succeed. They have to (1) take ownership of the strategy, (2) lead by example, and (3) make it happen. "Leaders," asserts Kelsch, "can be anywhere in the organization, but only those at the top can impact the entire organization and drive change through."

Leadership comes in many forms. Here are several examples:

- At Mt. Edgecumbe, leadership is Superintendent Larrae Rocheleau reconsidering his initial neutrality toward Quality, after having witnessed how its practice by a single teacher in one classroom energized his students.
- At Xerox, leadership is David Kearns rolling up his sleeves and participating in the same cascaded training sessions being provided to his entire organization. Highly visible as the chief cheerleader for change, Kearns not only "walked" but "taught" the talk.
- At Motorola, leadership *Six Sigma* style is a "way of life and acting," according to Bob Galvin. As CEO, he interviewed Motorola customers himself. Galvin also has been known to place Quality items first on senior management meeting agendas and to leave the meeting prior to the financial reports, resolute in his conviction that implementing TQM practices would achieve bottom-line results.
- At George Westinghouse VTHS, Total Quality leadership is total candor. It is Principal Lewis Rappaport admitting to his faculty when introducing them to TQM: "What we are doing is not working. It's my fault, but I need your help."

Leadership is often shared. It may be a Quality tag team, such as the guardian of the vision (Kearns) teamed with the master of implementation (Allaire). It may be one leader (Schargel) garnering external publicity to reinforce the internal change effort, while the other leader (Rappaport) stays closer to home, heading off potential roadblocks with the larger bureaucracy that might impede school-based improvement efforts. It may be affable veteran Millcreek Township Superintendent Bob Agnew teamed with his assistant superintendent, self-proclaimed "education terrorist" Verel Salmon. Or it may be low-key Superin-

tendent Larrae Rocheleau at Mt. Edgecumbe, teamed with
teacher and Deming missionary David Langford.

Leadership is a legacy. It is leaders, such as Kearns and
Galvin, who care enough about what occurs on their watch to
oversee a smooth transition to the next watch.

Leadership is for life. Continuous improvement personified
was reflected most sharply in our interview with Bob Galvin.
Although retired as CEO of Motorola, Galvin remains committed to Quality. He maintains an office and is active in the company. Currently, Galvin in the true spirit of *Six Sigma* is working
on a way to measure leadership so that the entire organization
can demonstrate such behavior. "'Anticipation' and 'commitment' are the two primary metrics of leadership," Galvin
explains, "anticipating what needs to be done and then committing to doing something about it." Organizations that successfully exercise leadership in the future will be those that
"anticipate correctly and act in a timely fashion." When asked
who he gets new ideas from, Galvin smiles and responds, "Everyone." With people as with organizations, lifelong learning is part
of being a lifelong leader.

Envisioning Something New

It is one thing for the leader to have a vision; it is quite another
for that vision to guide the behavior of an entire organization.
Leaders in successful Quality settings have been able to con-
ceptualize the theory in ways that translate into practice, steer
the change process, and guide their people in determining not
only how to perform their jobs, but even more important, what
those jobs should be.

In crafting their ideas on Quality, many of the leaders in
this study sought outside sustenance to bolster their internal for-
titude. They often came to TQM through the writings of the
gurus—Deming, Juran, Crosby. This is not so surprising in business, but it is no less true in education. The Wisconsin superintendents, Mt. Edgecumbe teacher David Langford, George Westinghouse assistant principal Franklin Schargel, Rappahannock
Superintendent David Gangel—all told us about how their "light
bulbs" flashed on when they read Deming's Fourteen Points or
attended subsequent TQM workshops. (See Appendix C for a list

of Deming's Fourteen Points.) Their hunger for information was satiated through additional readings, contact with Quality companies and consultants and their tools, and support from their membership or other professional associations.

In an effort to make the vision "real," these organizations may go out on the road. For example, just as David Kearns sent his troops to Fuji/Xerox in Japan, the Wisconsin Consortium sent curriculum directors and teachers to school districts in Johnson City (Upstate New York) and to Rochester, Minnesota, in order to witness outcome-based education in practice. "Seeing is believing" when it comes to most things, including implementing Quality or integrating it with other important education improvement efforts.

Moving from Outside to Inside

As the change process moves from conceptualization to implementation, organizations make several decisions to stay on track. If they started off on the wrong foot, our sites reworked their implementation plans. All ultimately designed their plans based on their own cultures, often with assistance from outside consultants. The sites' implementation plans were based on challenging goals that integrated the organizations' missions and priorities, with an eye on tackling priorities in manageable chunks.

Allowing for False Starts

"Two roads diverged in a wood," poet Robert Frost wrote, "and I, I took the one less traveled by and that has made all the difference."[1] Sometimes, too, as with Federal Express's early exposure to TQM, the road less traveled turns out to be the wrong road. "You can't take an outside Quality guru and slam dunk it," cautions Norman Rickard, Xerox's former vice president of Quality. "You need to combine your corporate culture with TQM." Problems may rest less with ideas than execution, as false starts often illustrate once organizations get back on course.

---

[1]"The Road Not Taken," from *The Poetry of Robert Frost*, ed., Edward Connery Lathen. Henry Holt & Co., Inc. (New York).

Home Growing the Implementation Plan . . .

It is not enough to have a vision that guides the change process. There also has to be a roadmap—an implementation plan—that lays out where organizations want to go (goals) and how to get there (strategies). If the vision is to be realized, it needs a way to connect, ultimately, to real work processes and real jobs. Although their plans ranged in the degree of detail and reflected different implementation strategies, all of the sites in this study had one thing in common. They did not farm out the responsibility for designing the plan. Whether creating a detailed business plan (Xerox), creating a cross-functional transition team (Vermont Department of Education), or following a less formal "play as you go" strategy (the Wisconsin Consortium)—in all cases the people assigned the task were those most familiar with the organization.

. . . But with a Little Bit of Help from Their Friends

Consultants, however, did play a key role in assisting these organizations to put their vision into operation. A certain breed of consultant is needed—individuals who are willing and able to take their customers' pulse and offer a prescription to fit their particular condition. A consultant's remedy should be designed to mesh with the corporate culture and advance the issues leadership deems important.

Experts in organizational development or statistical process control helped companies such as Xerox, Motorola, and Federal Express invent their TQM strategies. Consultants are often called on to assess the change process and, in the case of David Nadler at Xerox, serve as the CEO's alter ego. In some cases (Xerox, Federal Express), consultants become members of the organizational family, assisting in the transformation process over time.

Setting Challenging Goals

"If you don't know where you're going, you might not get there," to paraphrase the great American philosopher Yogi Berra. What is true in baseball is no less true in Quality. It is important to set lofty goals; otherwise TQM risks becoming an end in itself. And it is critical to define the goals clearly so that they motivate and rally people to make the needed changes.

The companies we visited established ambitious goals in order to prompt real improvements. Brenda Sumberg, director of Quality for Motorola University, explains why: "Leaders need to set unrealistically high goals that can only be accomplished through change and not just by doing the same things, only better." Adds Sumberg: "Next the organization has to provide the training and tools that enable employees to reach the goals and then get out of the way so they can."

There are no more ambitious goals than Motorola's *Six Sigma*, which "seeks perfection in everything we do." In 1981, following "The Big Bang," the company committed to a quality goal of ten times improvement in five years, one hundred times improvement in ten years, and *Six Sigma* capability (3.4 defects per million in each step of their work processes) by 1992. Some processes and products have achieved *Six Sigma*; others have not. In 1992, Motorola again upped the Quality ante by casting its next metrics in the billions. The new goals are tenfold improvement every two years, and ultimately twenty defects per billion in ten years.

Compared to the companies, the education sites have more general goals. All the sites are committed to the success of all children in safe environments. Many of their strategic plans mention Quality and continuous improvement as ways to achieve their goals. But their stated objectives are less quantifiable than those we found in business and, therefore, more difficult to measure. But so is the business they are in. Educators, however, can take comfort from the following advice, offered from an unexpected source. "The placement of the target is not as important as having a direction in which to aim," notes Bill Smith, "Father" of Motorola's *Six Sigma*.

Building on Priorities and Past Accomplishments

In all cases, the sites we studied are attempting to merge TQM implementation with their other priorities, both organizational and personal. In particular, they are forging linkages with two closely related factors. The first is what the organization is already trying to accomplish. Here are a few examples:

- Linkage to the school mission of Pacific Rim entrepreneurialism (Mt. Edgecumbe)
- Implementation of its long-term strategic plan (Vermont and Prince William County)
- Implementation of existing education priorities, such as school-based management (Prince William County), outcome-based education (the Wisconsin Consortium), and high-tech initiatives (Millcreek Township)
- A board directive to initiate significant change (Rappahannock and Brodhead School District in Wisconsin)

The second factor is what people already feel invested in and what is worth reinforcing. Examples include the following:

- A community-focus that broadens the definition of customer-focus (Globe Metallurgical and Vermont, whose communal sensibilities are best represented by ice cream moguls Ben and Jerry, the state's most famous ambassadors of TQM)
- A people-oriented culture (Federal Express, Motorola, George Westinghouse VTHS)
- Employee involvement and benchmarking (Xerox)

Focusing on Priorities . . .

Using TQM to focus on priorities rather than getting sidetracked by trivial issues characterizes the change strategies of these sites. As Xerox CEO Paul Allaire explains, "You want to have success and feel good, but you need to pick important issues to work on."

. . . But "Chunking" Priorities So as Not to Overwhelm Employees

At the same time, employees need a chance to practice new empowerment skills and behaviors without themselves being overpowered. Yet none of these organizations wants to waste its most valuable resource—its employees' time—on trivial problems. So a balance is reached. Employees address organizational priorities, but in manageable chunks. To illustrate: George Westinghouse faculty identified twenty-three priorities but started their continuous improvement effort by tackling the most important one—implementing a code of student conduct. Rappahannock conducted a survey to identify parent concerns and took action by addressing the most important problem—reducing discipline infractions on the buses.

Providing New Tools

If organizations and their people want to change behavior, they often need training on new ways to behave. The sites we visited provided customized training based on their respective organizational cultures and priorities. Equally important, they reinforced the training with opportunities for application.

Placing a Premium on Training

In transforming organizations, leaders cannot just say to their people, "Poof, you're empowered; now act differently." If they want their employees to manifest different behaviors, organizations have to provide them with roadmaps and support systems. The companies we visited all had a tradition of providing their employees with training. They assess professional development as an investment rather than a cost. Federal Express, for example, spends 3 percent of its annual sales on training. As a result, it already had extensive human resource capacity in place that could be used to develop its Quality curricula; the same was true of Xerox and Motorola. Even Globe Metallurgical, with only 265 employees, demonstrates a commitment to training. Globe has trained its employees (many of whom do not have college degrees or high school diplomas) to use statistical process controls so they can track their own work processes. Leaders in the education sites also placed great value on training as the primary means to change behavior and provided their people with the opportunity to learn new skills. They did so by conducting the training themselves or by actively recruiting outside assistance, primarily from Quality companies and consultants.

Providing Common Elements of Quality Training. . .

Quality training is very similar across all the company sites we visited. Courses tend to fall into two general categories.

- *TQM 101* is offered to employees throughout the companies. These courses generally consist of training in leading and participating in effective meetings (which maximize the use of time and result in good decisions); developing interactive skills that facilitate team building; using formal problem-solving processes to guide teams through decision making; employing Quality tools to collect, analyze, and act on customer-driven data; and using statistical process control techniques to track variation in and correct work processes.
- *Managing Quality* trains supervisors on how to be a successful supplier for their employees/customers. Courses are designed to help managers facilitate their employees' use of TQM 101, assess their progress and problems, provide support to enhance employee performance, reinforce desired behaviors, and anticipate future needs.

The larger companies—Motorola, Federal Express, and Xerox—continue to broaden the boundaries of the latter category, attempting to anticipate the needs of their managers as they move up and across the ranks and as their organizations decentralize line responsibilities. As a smaller company with fewer management levels and whose products are measurable combinations of raw materials, Globe tends to concentrate on the quantifiable side of TQM. In education, the Quality training generally was built around a business model (such as Xerox's *Leadership Through Quality*) or was self-taught from Deming's philosophy. Training in the use of Quality tools often was provided "just in time" as Quality Action Teams met to deal with specific issues.

. . . But Customizing Training Based on
Organizational Priorities and Realities

Where the contents of Quality training generally were consistent across the companies, how they offer that training—for whom and by whom—differs according to site.

- Although Xerox implemented *Leadership Through Quality* by decree (training was not voluntary for 100,000 employees), the end result has been employee empowerment. A top-down decision has led to bottom-up results, since Xerox employees now have a common decision-making language and are operating in self-managed cross-functional work teams in the field.
- Both Motorola and Federal Express pursued a more decentralized approach to training. The content is uniform within each company, but their business divisions determine when training should be offered and for whom. Motorola University, created in 1981, operates as a self-sustaining cost center. It offers a myriad of courses, but the business lines are free to purchase training from other sources as well.
- Given its small size, Globe Metallurgical has not developed its own Quality curriculum. By using Ford and General Motors supplier guidelines and certification standards, however, Globe has done the next best thing: borrowed from its customers.
- Training in the education sites took many forms, depending on existing priorities and resources. For example, the training tended to center on solving specific problems (Millcreek and Rappahannock); was cascaded (Vermont); or was integrated with other education priorities, such as outcome-based education (Wisconsin) or site-based management (Prince William).

Despite their differing training strategies, all four business sites we visited offered to train their own suppliers, in the name of providing customers with consistently high-quality products. Similarly, Rappahannock education leaders have trained parents and neighboring small businesses, and Vermont Department staff have trained their colleagues in the Department of Human Services.

Reinforcing Training in Application

The large companies in this study concluded that the key to sustaining the impact of training is to create their own training capacity. Thus, Xerox (even prior to implementation of *Leadership Through Quality*) built a corporate training center in Leesburg, Virginia. Motorola created Motorola University at its corporate headquarters in Schaumburg, Illinois. And Federal Express offers training through its Leadership Institute and the Quality Academy in Memphis, Tennessee. Their commitment does not end there, however. The companies also are taking steps to reinforce in *application* the skills learned in training. For example, Xerox assigns staff to assist its self-managed work teams in the field.

After application comes *evaluation*, which addresses the question of whether the training makes a difference. Motorola is attempting to provide the answer by applying *Six Sigma* metrics to its training efforts. Training programs are measured not just according to standard employee feedback surveys completed after training sessions (the approach taken by most organizations) but also by their impact on applying new skills on the job, which ultimately improves employee and organizational performance. Having made such a heavy investment in training, these companies are eager to see the returns. Providing adequate training resources is more of a challenge in education. Many educators are therefore dependent on companies for external training support and are eager to explore train-the-trainer models, so that they can institutionalize the training capacity internally.

Staying the Course

Organizations that implement Quality need time to institutionalize new behaviors and activities. Not surprisingly, in making changes our sites encountered skeptics along the way. Accordingly, they built in time for the new processes to show results. The successful alignment of Quality processes eventually enabled all employees as part of their normal course of work to participate actively in building a high-performance organization.

Putting the Pieces Together

Creating opportunities to apply, reinforce, and institutionalize new behaviors: that is the challenge once initial TQM training has been provided. One of the main reasons we included the companies in this study was the opportunity to benchmark successful practices of organizations that have been using TQM for a relatively long period of time. We initially assumed that the information would be useful to educators (and other organizations, too) eager for role models. Experience has validated our initial assumption. Not all companies do all things, but an amalgamation of their successful practices would look like this:

- Translating the organization's core values, vision, and mission into language and priorities that motivate all employees and focus their work
- Setting challenging goals in measurable terms—and then measuring progress
- Developing a common decision-making language by training in family units and applying problem-solving techniques in cross-functional teams
- Building a permanent training capacity
- Creating a Quality infrastructure to assess needs and progress throughout the organization
- Integrating Quality practices into key support systems, work processes, and incentives—rewards, promotions, and performance evaluations—that reinforce desired behaviors and outcomes
- Celebrating risk taking and successes
- Using organizational self-assessments, such as the Baldrige Award Criteria or equivalents, to sustain the change effort and identify new improvement opportunities
- Seeking ways to become better by benchmarking the organization's products, services, and practices against industry

leaders, not only within each industry but across organizational sectors
- Analyzing and sharing experiences, good and bad, as a continuous improvement strategy
- Providing for smooth leadership transitions

How do you know when "you get it"? Perhaps the best answer comes from Xerox employees up and down the organization. When asked how one can be assured whether TQM has taken hold, time and again their reply was: when someone coming in from the outside would have trouble uprooting it. Thus, as difficult as Quality is to implement, there is a silver lining. Once the critical changes have occurred, natural skepticism works in an organization's favor to sustain them.

Anticipating the Skeptics and Buying the Time

In many ways, TQM runs counter to an American culture that demands instant gratification. TQM, by definition, is after all a long-term (that is, continuous) improvement process. All the sites in this study agreed that time was needed to demonstrate favorable bottom-line results. And companies such as Xerox, which used *Leadership Through Quality* to transform its own corporate culture, build in the required time for TQM to take root.

Longevity is not yet a burning issue for the education sites, given the relative infancy of their Quality initiatives. Even they, however, recognize the need eventually to justify their efforts, if for no other reason than the substantial amount of time for planning, training, and team decision making they are asking from their staffs. Building in time to show results is difficult, primarily because of the initial skepticism that accompanies most change efforts. And with good reason. Many people in our sites were leery of TQM at first, based not so much on the ideas as on their previous encounters with change efforts. Presidential Review Manager Ron Peer summarizes the typical employee concerns he remembers at Xerox: "I don't have time; this stuff never works; it's here today, gone tomorrow; it's the best flavor of the month."

Skepticism can occur at the highest organizational levels as well. When asked about the initial reaction of his senior executives at Federal Express to Quality, CEO Fred Smith answered with the numbers: "Five of the ten were true believers, 25 percent took some convincing, and 25 percent never got there and eventually went somewhere else." And for the skeptics who remain cynics, "you may eventually have to legislate it," adds Edith Kelly, Federal Express's vice president of Quality.

Recognizing That Quality Is Continuous—That It Is Forever

This chapter has focused on the how's of implementing TQM. Accordingly, it has highlighted the *human aspects* of Quality: the personal and the situational, the unique mix of different individuals within different contexts, and the training and incentives that enable all employees to contribute to improving their own organizations. Implementing TQM requires change, and only people can make change happen. The more you learn, the more you learn you need to do. The more you do, the more you want to improve. As Beloit Turner Superintendent Chuck Melvin says: "The more I get into this stuff, the more interesting I find it." Thus, for people truly committed to running a Quality organization, only an Act of God (as in Xerox's Total Satisfaction Guarantee) is likely to dissuade them from trying.

Chapter 5

Educational Applications

Chapter Five describes some of what we saw and heard about Quality on our visits to the seven education sites. Our intended outcome is for the reader to understand better what TQM looks like when forward-thinking educators adapt new ways of assessing, planning, and doing their business to improve student and system performance.

We selected the Malcolm Baldrige National Quality Award Criteria as a way of organizing this chapter because the categories are being used increasingly by private sector and public sector organizations as a self-assessment tool. The company sites used the Baldrige Criteria to compete for and win the award. Most sites also are using them after the award process to continue improvement efforts. Some of the education sites—specifically, Rappahannock County and Millcreek Township—are also using the Baldrige Criteria to assess and measure their progress. In fact, all of the sites we visited used some form of self-assessment to establish baseline data and to measure their progress regularly.

The Baldrige Criteria are grouped into seven categories, with the overriding goal being "the delivery of ever-improving value to a customer." The categories[1] are:

[1] In the introduction to each category, we cite the definition included in the Baldrige Award Criteria. We modified them slightly by substituting *organiza-*

- Leadership
- Information and Analysis
- Strategic Quality Planning
- Human Resource Development and Management
- Management of Process Quality
- Quality and Operational Results
- Customer Focus and Satisfaction

Figure 5.1 illustrates how these seven categories form a system framework. Senior executive *leadership* is the "driver" of the system. Leaders create the values, goals, and work systems and guide the sustained pursuit of customer value and improvement in organizational performance.

"The system" is a set of well-defined and integrated processes designed to meet customer, quality, and performance requirements: (1) the use of *information and analysis* in making critical organizational decisions; (2) reliance on *strategic planning* in identifying and implementing organizational priorities; (3) the development and management of *human resources*; and (4) the *management of quality processes*, which essentially aligns all of the organizational pieces. The driver and the system focus on two key interrelated performance indicators: *achieving results* and *satisfying customers*. They do this by setting the "goal" of delivering ever-improving value to customers and by agreeing on "measures of progress" to achieve results.

An important caveat: None of the education sites in this study consistently exhibited *all* of the Baldrige Criteria. All of the sites exhibited some, however, and all used the criteria as benchmarks for the systems they planned to create. Because the sites are so different, their Quality practices also vary, reflecting their respective leadership styles, organizational priorities and settings, and community demographics. Our intent is to high-

---

tion for *company*, so that the categories would more appropriately fit an education setting. Further extrapolation of the Baldrige Criteria for education organizations is documented in the *Total Quality Management Handbook*, prepared by On Purpose Associates and distributed by the American Association of School Administrators.

Figure 5.1   Baldrige Award Criteria Framework: Dynamic Relationships.

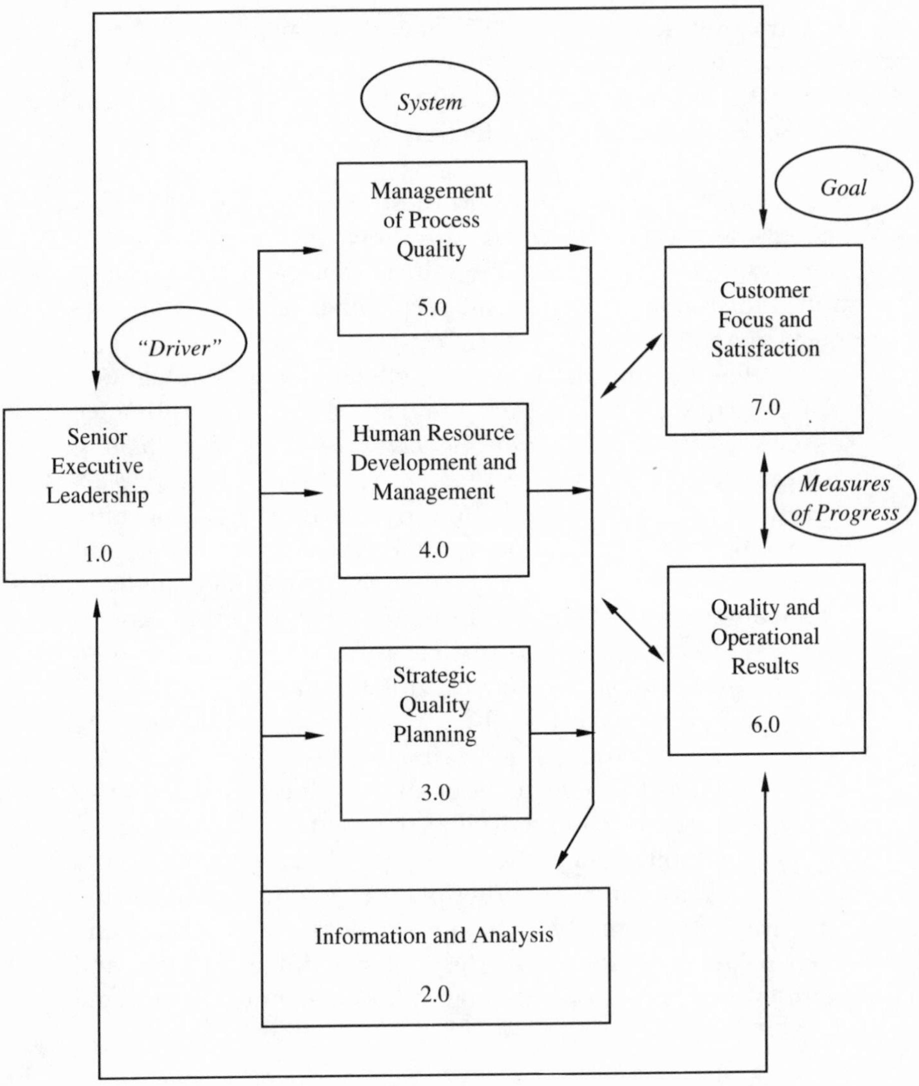

Source: Adapted from the Malcolm Baldrige National Quality Award, 1993 Award Criteria.

light some examples of what Quality in education looks like in "real life."

Leadership

> Baldrige definition: The *Leadership* Category examines senior executives' *personal* leadership and involvement in creating and sustaining a customer focus and clear and visible quality values. Also examined is how the quality values are integrated into the organization's management system and reflected in the manner in which the organization addresses its public responsibilities and corporate citizenship.

As Richard P. Mills, Commissioner of Education, Vermont, said: "The Commissioner's role is to be a visionary—to be like a laser and burn away everything extraneous."

The role of the leaders is radically different in Quality organizations than in traditional organizations. Gone is the culture where employees must guess what will please their immediate boss and ultimately the CEO. Everyone recognizes they have a new boss now—the customer. Under TQM, the leader's role is one of enabling everyone in the organization to focus on pleasing the customer. This means that the leader develops work processes, goals, and measurements. It is the leader who sees to it that everyone has a sense of how important a particular task or project is to accomplishing the goals. The leader, then, must reflect an understanding of the mission, vision, and values of the organization in order to demonstrate them to everyone else. The leader must also ensure that others have the same vision, so that they can "hit the road" running.

Reflections of a Leader

David Gangel, superintendent of Rappahannock County Public Schools, is described by his staff as having vision and leadership qualities. He began applying Quality techniques throughout his school district after reading about and attending training on TQM. "It felt right with my perspective of how education should be," explains Gangel. So he cultivated support from his board of education to bring Quality to Rappahannock County. He applied for and was accepted into training sponsored by the Virginia State Department of Education and the Xerox Corporation. It entitled the superintendent, the assistant superintendent, and some of the teaching staff to attend Xerox's *Leadership Through Quality* training.

Gangel's personal credo is to model behaviors he wants everyone to exhibit. He insists this is one way to foster trust. And it has worked. Teachers, administrators, parents, support staff, and board members notice and appreciate his example. Using Quality techniques, the district has developed a mission statement, because, as Gangel asks, "How can you ask people to change if they don't know what they're changing to?" Gangel has been trained by Xerox staff as a trainer; he has trained others in the district, as well as some small businesses in the community. A passage from Rappahannock's Continuous Improvement plan sums up Gangel's attitude and behavior: "Board members and Instructional Leaders—Superintendent, Assistant Superintendent, Building Principals and Assistants—have the power to create an atmosphere in which excellence will thrive. Such an atmosphere will contain not only emphasis on . . . competencies and skills, but also on forbearance, kindness, and mutual respect. The latter intangible qualities are among those which inspire trust and esprit de corps, without which little real progress is possible. The extent to which excellence and improvement exist, emerge, and continue depends on the quality of leadership."

Redefining the Role of the Leader

In traditional organizations, regardless of the boss's admonitions about "being part of the team," there is always a strong sense of who is really in charge and who must ultimately be pleased. In the education sites we visited, these lines of authority were less distinct. Leaders had redefined their roles to include sharing their decision-making authority. They worked to refocus everyone's attention, including their own, on how to satisfy their customers.

This was particularly evident in an Oregon, Wisconsin Curriculum Coordination Council (CCC) meeting. This fifteen-member cross-functional team included Linda Barrows, the district superintendent, as well as teachers, administrators, and a board member. The first evidence of Quality was that the meeting began on time. The second was the well-planned agenda, with the person responsible for and allotted time noted beside each item. Keeping to the agenda, the CCC openly discussed its progress toward outcome-based education, the curriculum revisions that had taken place, and the successes and limitations of its work. The discussion included some of their individual and collective frustrations, with a focus on resolution of problems. They all agreed with one team member's observation: "We've moved to the point where we can't go back to where we were, but we need restructuring to occur before we can move forward." Most striking was Barrows's complete participation in the discussion and the CCC's obvious comfort with her involvement. A freewheeling discussion with a CEO present does not happen in traditional organizations. Yet it was happening here. Without knowing titles beforehand, it would have been a challenge to identify people's job responsibilities, let alone single out the superintendent, in this meeting.

Board Leadership: Support for Change

The Southwestern Wisconsin Quality Consortium is unusual in many ways. Not only have the five superintendents coalesced to pool their knowledge, resources, and staffs, but their respective boards of education have also presented a united front to help promote Quality throughout their districts and the State of Wisconsin. They have made presentations throughout the state to ensure that Quality as a tool for change is understood and fostered.

These boards did not necessarily accept the notion of change without some convincing. Steve Ashmore, superintendent of the Brodhead Public Schools, indicated that during a district vision-setting meeting early in the process, concern was expressed over these statements—"becoming a leading school district" and "all students being successful." After much discussion, he said: "Okay, I'll start the year by telling the staff that we

want most, but not all, of the students to be successful, and that
we want to be an okay school system, not a leading school system."
It did not take long for a board member to speak up and say that
they were there to give the best to *all* children. According to Ashmore, "The vision ended up firmly grounded in policy."

Developing a Leadership Team

Sometimes the superintendent of schools leads the Quality
effort personally and gains support from another "believer." Or
the superintendent may be introduced to TQM by someone else
in the district, who then plays a role in the development and
implementation plans. Regardless of who finds it first, a team
evolves, nourished by the trust the players have in one another.
Typically, one person takes the lead and the other plays a seemingly more supportive role, with the support role considered to
be just as important in terms of strategy and implementation.
We saw several examples of leadership teams. The following are
a few of the highlights.

Rappahannock County Public Schools. David Gangel is
joined by Bob Chappell, assistant superintendent, in modeling
Quality in the Rappahannock Schools. Chappell accompanied
Gangel to the original Xerox training, and he has been a facili-
tator in many of the district's cross-functional problem-solving
teams. Representing a consistent presence in the central office,
Chappel and Gangel share a commitment to ensuring the success of Quality in the Rappahannock Schools. The district's staff,
teachers, parents, and board members depend on the knowledge and experience of their two administrators. They look to
them confidently for continuing and strengthening their quality
initiatives.

George Westinghouse VTHS. Lewis Rappaport and Franklin Schargel are principal and assistant principal, respectively, at
George Westinghouse VTHS. They worked successfully together in other New York City schools in the 1970s. When Rappaport
became principal at Westinghouse seven years ago, he began
with a mission of changing the culture and performance in the
inner-city high school and invited Schargel to join him.

Both are lifelong learners, committed to continuously
improving education for urban youngsters. They share a long

history of working together and, most important, they trust one another. Therefore, when Schargel began his reading about Quality and asked to attend a national meeting on the subject sponsored by GOAL/QPC, Rappaport enthusiastically supported him. Schargel credits that meeting with completely changing his attitude about schools. He began to devise plans for introducing Quality to Westinghouse. Rappaport not only supported Schargel, but he began to immerse himself in the process as well.

As a result, the two high school leaders are now working with staff, parents, and students to apply the Quality tools to some of the schools' problems. They have worked to reduce the number of students who fail all of their classes from 151 to 11, increase membership in the Parent-Teachers' Association from 12 in 1987 to 250 in 1991, and establish interdepartmental meetings for the first time.

They are co-leaders, although their personal styles are very different. Rappaport is the more "laid back" member of the duo; Schargel is the "showman." Their different approaches have allowed them to accomplish several things simultaneously. For example, Schargel has brought national attention to the school by writing articles, pursuing Quality companies for their support, and speaking at national and local meetings. Rappaport accompanies Schargel on some of his speaking engagements, but he continues to "mind the store" and support the change process at the school.

Millcreek Township. Robert Agnew, superintendent, and Verel Salmon, assistant superintendent, have forged a team in Millcreek Township, Pennsylvania, which surrounds Erie on three sides. Agnew has been in the district since 1968 and superintendent for eleven years. Agnew and Salmon have worked together in Millcreek for the past nine years. Based on a long-term commitment to high-quality education, a history of teacher professionalism, and the trusting relationship the two have developed over the years, introducing Quality to the district was a logical transition. Salmon's first exposure to Quality began when he was a science student in college. He observes that "the connections of Quality to K–12 education were obvious." With encouragement from Agnew, he is supported internally in his efforts to implement Quality inside Millcreek and externally by the community of Erie's parallel venture into Quality via the Erie Excellence Council.

Salmon has played the role of "quality muse" throughout Millcreek for the past six to eight years. He has accomplished the following:

- Formed Quality teams of administrators and teachers and brought in Quality consultants to train them in the tools and processes.
- Formed a team of central office secretaries and assisted them in using some of the Quality tools. They won one of the 1992 Erie Excellence Council's Quality Awards.
- Continued to offer Quality training as part of the professionals' "menu" of in-service training.
- Arranged with local businesses (Lord Corporation, American Sterilization, International Paper, and Eriez Magnetics) to open their training to Millcreek staff.
- Served as chair of the Erie Excellence Council's academic committee since its inception in 1986.
- Utilized TQM techniques—for example, nominal group techniques on major factors—to discuss year-long schools with community groups.

Agnew's support and involvement have bolstered these efforts. In fact, the team they have forged was a strong factor in helping the district win the highest Quality Award from the Erie Excellence Council in 1992, after it went head to head with Quality companies and organizations throughout the Erie region. But the superintendent insists on giving credit where it is due: "It's Verel who has kept the quality movement alive and flourishing in Millcreek."

Mt. Edgecumbe High School. Larrae Rocheleau, superintendent, and David Langford, teacher, say they could not have accomplished what they did without the other's involvement and support. After Langford "discovered" Quality and gained Rocheleau's commitment to proceed with training students and staff, the two became a two-person information and support network. They began by sharing books and videos they had purchased or borrowed, as well as the insight of people with whom they talked and had meetings.

They team taught a college course to teachers, people from a small college in Sitka, and the Coast Guard; each took half the class and helped the other prepare his lessons. Both went to Juneau at the request of the Commissioner of Education to conduct approximately 1,000 person-hours of training at the State Department of Education. In addition, they taught individual college classes; Langford taught classes at the hospital and Rocheleau at the Coast Guard. Even with their separate teaching loads, they continued to consult and support the other's efforts.

(Note: Since our visit, both David Langford and Larrae Rocheleau have left Mt. Edgecumbe High School. One goal for the new staff is to continue the tradition of sharing responsibility for and supporting efforts in Quality.)

Practicing Good Citizenship and Public Responsibility

Mt. Edgecumbe prides itself on being an active member of the Sitka community. One of its most important contributions is its knowledge and use of Quality. An early entrepreneurial business venture had been very successful—the students smoked, packaged, and sold fish to Japanese companies. The school was ready to form a different kind of business with a local Quality company, so they advertised for a partner in the newspaper. They selected a seafood distributor, and together they decided to establish Alaskan Harvest, a fresh fish mail order company. (Their goal: To become the "L. L. Bean of fresh fish.") When we visited, some students were in the throes of developing a business plan. A student-developed Business Partnership Relations Diagram includes a breakdown of individuals' tasks, the classes in which each activity will take place, the resources for funding the project, and so on, fully integrating the company into the students' school plan.

Information and Analysis

Baldrige definition: The *Information and Analysis* Category examines the scope, validity, analysis, management, and use of data and information to drive quality excellence and to improve opera-

tional and competitive performance. Also examined is the adequacy of the organization's data,
information, and analysis system to support
improvement of the organization's customer focus,
products, services, and internal operations.

Charles A. Melvin III, of the School District of Beloit
Turner noted: "Using statistics is new to schools. Some people
use numbers to punish, rather than as a way to change the belief
system."

Using Data to Improve Work Processes

Millcreek Township is trying to measure as much as possible to
make their district the best it can be. The extensive data collection and analysis performed by the school district assist them in
making decisions for continuous improvement. Included are
food service customer surveys, formal and informal administrative classroom visitations, item analysis of achievement tests, a
computer-based learning management system for quality assurance, the school-based long-range-plan yearly updates, and the
reading specialists' quality monitoring procedures. Verel Salmon
insists: "By using data, excellent organizations can keep moving,
keep improving."

Millcreek also benchmarks its quality processes against
private companies, making a conscious effort to identify and
make team visits to several institutions each year. Locally, they
have selected Eriez Magnetics, American Sterilization, and
Morris Coupling; nationally, they have visited Motorola and
Westinghouse. "If we hear about innovative programs, we try to
travel there," says Salmon. "We want to learn all we can about
their programs, from little things like congratulatory banners in
an individual plant, to big things, like their overall strategies and
techniques for presenting their training."

Students Using Data to Track Their Own Learning

The students at Mt. Edgecumbe High School are serious about
their education. They think about and accept responsibility for

becoming lifelong learners. In return, they expect their teachers and the school to provide state-of-the-art equipment, teaching techniques, and opportunities to learn as much and as well as they can. Students are taught how to use the Quality process tools to solve problems, and some of the classes begin with a discussion of objectives for which they reach consensus. Few of their classes use traditional textbooks.

In the technology applications class that we observed, students wrote their autobiographies as though they were living in the year 2020. Using actuarial tables, labor statistics, and other data, they projected their life-styles, their occupations, their living arrangements, and their major possessions, including how they would pay for them. At first, the students had themselves living life-styles of the rich and famous—owning expensive homes, driving fancy sports cars, traveling worldwide. Information is power, but in this case, sobering. Data from the Bureau of Labor Statistics and other sources became a reality check. Once they applied some of their mathematics skills, such as computing their income tax, mortgage interest, and checking accounts, they were taken aback by the amount of money they would have to earn in order to subsidize that life-style. And it underscored the value of an education for supporting the style to which they hoped to become accustomed. Their final autobiographies represented optimistic, yet more realistic notions of how they would be living in the year 2020. "This exercise helped us to see what we have to do to become the kinds of adults we want to be," one student assessed.

Some Mt. Edgecumbe classes have been reconfigured to allow students to track their own learning progress rather than waiting for teachers to evaluate them using traditional standardized tests and grades. David Langford, Mt. Edgecumbe teacher, developed a six-level matrix based on a learning skills hierarchy. Beginning with "Level I: Knowledge," students demonstrate competencies on a continuum through "Level II: Understanding/Comprehension," "Level III: Application," "Level IV: Analysis," "Level V: Synthesis," and, finally, "Level VI: Appreciation/Evaluation." To receive credit for a course, student competencies must be demonstrated at 100 percent in the knowledge-level outcomes, at 90 percent at the comprehension-level outcomes, and at 90 percent of the application-level out-comes. Students assess their own progress on a competency matrix form developed by Langford. The forms also include the admonition: Competency is not easily forgotten!

Using Information to Improve Student Performance

We discovered many examples of how information is being used to bolster student performance.

Parkview School District. In 1987, Parkview secondary staff (grades seven to twelve) were frustrated by low standard-ized test scores, especially in tenth-grade math. They were also disturbed by the 29 percent failure rate among their students, which they defined as the percentage of all students who received at least one F in a grading period. The staff had spent several years attempting to turn this failure rate around, with a particular focus on curriculum and teaching training. But their efforts had proved fruitless. The principals and superintendent identified solving the failure rate and test score problems as their top priority.

The district formed a Parkview Leadership Group, which included elementary and secondary staff, to address these and other perceived problems in the district. In 1988–89, they began to identify the root causes of the failure rate in grades seven to twelve, singling out undone homework as a major cause of fail-ure. They implemented a series of procedures, including an after-school, ninth-period "homework period," and scheduled a bus to be available for those students; peer tutoring; a remedia-tion period for academic teachers to replace some of their non-classroom duties; and a homework policy, passed by the board of education. By the end of the school year, the failure rate had declined by over 50 percent as compared to the year before.[2]

In the spirit of continuous improvement, the Leadership Group began studying outcome-based education during the 1989–90 school year. All staff participated in a day-long

[2]Technically, most of the remaining paragraphs of this section would be found in Category 6.0, "Results," of the Baldrige Criteria. They are placed here to illustrate the impact of using information to tackle priorities.

awareness-building activity in November, and half of the district teachers were trained in "mastery learning." All of the academic teachers were assigned a remediation period at the end of the school day. As a result of these activities, the failure rate declined an additional 10 percent, the honor roll membership increased by 50 percent (from 1987); and students attending postsecondary education rose to 84 percent (from 60 percent in 1987).

During the 1990–91 school year, the leadership group led the district to commit to the transformation to outcome-based education. The district also formed its consortium with three other districts, all committed to the belief that learner outcomes and aligned assessments were the way to ensure students' success. At that point in time, TQM was built into the transforming system by aligning with standards associated with the goal of continuous improvement. Quality Improvement "basic training" was provided for the leaders from all consortium school leaders, including Ishikawa, Pareto charts, and flowcharts. As a result of this continued focus on outcome-based education, the failure rate of the grade-seven-to-twelve cadre declined by 68 percent and discipline referrals dropped 40 percent, as compared to 1990.

During the 1991–92 school year, the transformation process continued and student performance continued to improve. The grade-seven-to-twelve group's failure rate declined 73 percent and discipline referral declined to almost 60 percent, relative to 1987. In addition, project teams were created to develop plans for preschool programs, district budget cuts, and prekindergarten and family education. The results included a full-day every day kindergarten and an alliance with a community group for Quality child care. A Headstart program has been initiated in the school building, support services are available for children up to eighteen years of age, and a Homework and Extended Opportunities Policy has been adopted for kindergarten through grade six.

Christa McAuliffe School, Prince William County, Virginia. The Christa McAuliffe School is one of three pilot schools in the countywide district using Quality to implement the district's site-based management mandate. Staff at this K–5 school apply and model Quality processes through their cross-functional Quality

Council and in many of their classrooms. These elementary
school teachers now look at their colleagues who teach the next
higher grades—including the teachers at the middle school—
as one set of customers. They work to coordinate their curricula
to ensure that they, as suppliers, are meeting these customers'
needs. They are also listening much more carefully to the parents and to the students. The result is that the teachers have said
that they feel as though they are "pulling together" now.

In selected activities, kindergarten classes are using modified Quality processes, like the nominal group techniques (a
brainstorming activity in which participants vote on and rank a
number of issues) to make group decisions. Students are encouraged to work cooperatively in teams; they have instituted a buddy
system where older students are working with the younger ones,
enabling both partners to feel successful. Second graders are
applying meeting skills in their small groups as each group member is assigned a role and the roles are then rotated within the
groups. One McAuliffe teacher observed: "Younger children can
make decisions for themselves. They are learning how to take
responsibility for themselves. They know what they do well, and
what they can do better." Fourth- and fifth-grade students at
McAuliffe are using brainstorming and other tools to analyze
problems before they start to solve them. Students in all grades
work with their teachers to establish individual measurable goals;
work jointly selected by the students and teachers is then placed
in their portfolios for authentic assessment. One teacher
explains: "The process skills keep the kids focused and save us all
time in the long run."

Noninstructional Applications

We encountered many noninstructional applications of TQM.
School District of Beloit Turner. All staff in the Beloit Turner district are serious about their roles in making the schools
better for everyone, especially the students. The custodial staff
is considered to be an important contributor to that outcome.
Tom Brooks, a graduate of the Beloit Turner schools, was hired
as director of building and grounds in December 1991. His job

is to manage the twelve-person custodial staff. Shortly after he joined the district, he began his classes in TQM through the University of Wisconsin. As a result of his coursework, combined with his predilection for involving staff in decision making, Brooks has been encouraging the staff to collect and use data supplied by the school staff that will improve the custodial staff's customer service. His predecessor's managerial training and style reflected the older, more traditional "control from the top" approach, which discouraged staff from voicing opinions or offering suggestions for improvement. As a result, Brooks has been focusing on opening communications and encouraging the staff to come up with some alternative ideas for doing their jobs and pleasing their customers—for example, using one cleaning product instead of three.

Being the first to bring Quality management techniques to the job has been "interesting," according to Brooks. "Many of the people on my staff didn't graduate from high school. They aren't very good readers. They weren't sure what to think about some of the ideas I was suggesting to them. Plus, the kind of boss they had before didn't help things much." Rather than giving them books and articles to read, Brooks talked with his staff and used real-life examples of how Quality techniques could be infused into their jobs. His efforts have paid off mightily. He helped his staff develop a faculty survey to help them understand their customers and revise their work processes. Specifically, they asked their customers to evaluate their maintenance performance in the following areas: classrooms, rest rooms, carpeting, offices, lounges, locker rooms, gyms, cafeterias, and hallways. All were scored above average for levels of satisfaction. Brooks graphed the findings, which showed that the staff gave the best, most immediate service to certain areas—classrooms, rest rooms, and carpeted areas.

The custodial staff was delighted to receive the enormous praise that was generated by the survey. Sadly, they had never received this kind of feedback before. Their pleasure at feeling as though they are making positive contributions to their school district has encouraged them to continue their Quality efforts with renewed enthusiasm. His staff's well-earned success shapes

Brooks's advice to other school districts: "There has to be some
means for non-instructional folks to be involved in this kind of
change process. It doesn't have to be terribly academic. They
can understand and use surveys if they're explained appropriately. Then they can use the data from the surveys to make decisions about how they do their jobs better."

Brooks's summary of the customer surveys included
graphs and Pareto charts. He wrote, "To get all of our processes
under control will require the Custodial Department to remove
the variance in our use of equipment, supplies, and procedures. . . . This survey gives the Custodial Department a base line
for gauging the results of these planned actions. Because the
action we take is dependent on the information we receive
through these surveys, it is our hope that you will be understanding and cooperative in our future survey efforts."

Rappahannock County Public Schools. The Rappahannock County Public Schools survey parents annually to assess
customers' needs in such areas as academic rigor/challenge,
courtesy, related services (such as cafeteria, transportation),
and communication. The 1991 survey identified a big customer
concern—school bus discipline problems. Bob Chappell, assistant superintendent, created a cross-functional problem-solving
team that included bus drivers.

At first glance, it seemed as though purchasing more
buses was the only answer. But that proved not to be the case.
Using various problem-solving tools, the team carefully tracked
the point at which discipline problems appeared. The results
indicated that problems began when there were over forty-five
students on the bus. (A full-length bus has a sixty-four-passen-
ger capacity but holds forty-four comfortably with only two children in a seat.) The team met five times to determine the
source of discipline referrals. They tallied them by bus size to
test the hypothesis from several drivers that making bus loads
smaller would reduce the problems. The team recommended
additional routes, reduced numbers of students on a bus at any
one time, and reduced time spent on the bus—all considered
to be root causes for the discipline problems. They came up
with five options to recommend, ranging in cost from $15,000

to $107,000, depending on whether they purchased new equipment, hired additional personnel, and so on. (At the time of our visit, the options had been offered to the superintendent, but no final decision had been made yet.) Dan Keyser, one of the two bus drivers on the committee, saw value in participating in solving a problem in which he is a player. He further explains: "It makes you understand the system better, because you see that everyone is part of a whole. If you're affected by the problem, you should be part of the system that solves the problem."

Strategic Quality Planning

> Baldrige definition: The *Strategic Quality Planning* Category examines the organization's planning process and how all key quality requirements are integrated into overall business planning. Also examined are the organization's short- and longer-term plans and how quality and operational performance requirements are deployed to all work units.

The vision statement of the School District of Brodhead reads as follows: "We want to develop local processes, policies, governance structures, instructional strategies, and design that will enable our school district to utilize W. Edwards Deming's 'Total Quality Management' approach. Deming's principles offer us an overall organizational philosophy and environment that support nationally validated practices such as . . . Outcomes Based Learning, . . . Mastery Learning, and . . . Effective Schools' research."

Several of the education sites that we visited had devised strategic plans that required changes in their priorities and in the basic ways in which they were going to conduct all their business. In some cases, the plans preceded the sites' introduction to or involvement with Quality; in others, TQM was used as a way to bring their education communities together to develop the plan. Sometimes they applied the principles of Quality without even realizing they were practicing it.

The Strategic Plan—Then TQM

Sometimes the strategic plan comes first, with Quality being introduced later.

   Vermont Department of Education. In 1991, Vermont developed its *Green Mountain Challenge: Very High Skills for Every Student; No Exception, No Excuses* as a five-year plan for transforming the education system throughout the state. Rick Mills, the state's commissioner of education, worked with educators and interested citizens statewide to write four Education Goals, with high expectations for all students. Local communities have the option of further heightening the goals to reflect their own priorities. The plan also calls for defining a common core of learning, expanding assessment, and ultimately restructuring all aspects of the education delivery system, including the state's Department of Education.

   The department's restructuring effort drove their decision to adopt Quality, once they realized they required a different organizational culture to facilitate the changes of their new work environment. Intended to complement the changes that were occurring in the state's various local districts, the department established new teams with "internal" and "external" managers. In the process of devising and implementing these departmentwide reforms, the commissioner and some of the department staff ascertained that a change in the organization's culture was necessary if the new structure was to be successful. Quality was selected as the process that would meld the culture change with the restructuring plan. Technical support would be provided by Norm Deets and John Foley, two former Xerox executives now working with education institutions under the auspices of the National Center on Education and the Economy.

   At the time of our visit, there was a flurry of activity. The department restructuring plan was just being implemented concurrent with TQM training for staff. In-house trainers had been fully trained in the Xerox tools and processes. Training had been rolled out during the summer of 1992, beginning with the commissioner and top managers. Many of the staff were enthusiastic about TQM as a tool that would provide them with a focus to better serve their customer. Some staff, however, did not see the difference between what they had been doing in the past ("We've always worked collaboratively and focused on customers") and what they were being asked to do in the new iteration. Nonetheless, most of the people we interviewed saw TQM's greatest potential as a way of planning and implementing the department's restructuring. They advised that once the reorganization was put in place, employees should be trained in their new family (work) groups.

Prince William County. With 44,000 students, Prince William County is the third largest school district in the Commonwealth of Virginia. A "bedroom community" of Washington, D.C., the district continues to grow. Currently, there are sixty-one schools, nine of which have been added in the past five years.

Edward Kelly has been superintendent of schools for the past five years. He described his own development toward employee empowerment and self-managed work teams as emanating from the Effectiveness Training he received in the early and mid 1980s. With Kelly's input and guidance, the board of education has developed a strategic plan that includes fourteen five-year measurable goals to improve education and to support its mission statement that all children can learn. (The goals address such issues as grade-level achievement, reduced dropout rates, no discrepancies among minorities, and so on.) The plan specifies school-based management for each of the district's schools, and each school is to develop a plan for attaining the district's fourteen goals.

To facilitate the mandate of school-based management, the district is adopting Quality as a process for change. They selected three pilot schools—an elementary, middle, and high school—to attend Xerox's *Leadership Through Quality* (TQM) training under the auspices of a Virginia Department of Education grant. The superintendent, key central office staff, and the principal plus one key teacher from each of the pilot schools attended the training. The district is also developing in-house training capabilities at its central office to train other staff as well as the pilot sites' administrators, teachers, community advisory councils, and nonteaching staff. Eventually, the training will be provided to all of the district's 7,500 employees; ideally, there will be a trainer in each school building.

The pilot schools are working toward integrating the principles and tools of Quality into their everyday activities. Christa McAuliffe, the pilot elementary school, has been particularly successful in applying TQM. Its first TQM activity was to engage its advisory council in developing a schoolwide plan for accomplishing site-based management. "They told us to start with a small problem as our first activity," explains Robin Sweeney, principal. "In retrospect, the school plan *was* a pretty big task. But we knew we had to come up with the plan at some point in time. And how better to learn site-based management than by doing it?" The advisory council now uses the Xerox problem-solving processes, effective meeting skills, and interactive skills as a matter of course.

TQM—Then the Strategic Plan

Some organizations adopt TQM first, then create a strategic plan.

    School District of Brodhead. Brodhead's *Restructuring Blueprint* is a five-year plan that was developed by TQM, of TQM, and for TQM. With a focus on the student as customer, Brodhead has revised its management, operational systems, and board policies to meet student learning needs. Using Quality principles, the district assembled a network that includes representation from the school district, its surrounding community, the state department of education, local businesses, state universities, an ecological consulting firm, and Quality consultants to develop their plan. Part of the plan was developed as a part of their work within the Southwestern Wisconsin Quality Consortium; district staff developed part on their own. Emphasis is on the school building as the site for innovative strategies, with support from the district's administration. District employees spent time developing Quality indicators, which have created a common language for all employees. Shared decision making will extend to the budget process, which will include development of a management system for categorical funding that is focused on student outcomes.

    The introduction to the district's *Restructuring Blueprint* includes this statement:

The staff, Board, and community have spent the last two years examining and developing their vision for a quality school. We have reached a critical mass of staff and school board who believe we need to change our structure and need processes to develop and implement:

- a new vision for reform
- new organizational designs
- a practitioners' design that is developed by staff utilizing validated practices
- a structure that has extensive support to promote maximum student learning opportunities
- a Win/Win learning environment for students, staff, parents, and community
- a world class quality school which meets national education goals

The *Restructuring Blueprint* provides operational plans for implementing the vision. True to TQM principles, it also includes an internal and external evaluation system and a means to test the product design.

Belle Valley School, Millcreek Township. The process for planning the Belle Valley School is mentioned earlier in the Millcreek case study. More about the school—and why it is considered to be a model facility—is worth including. Describing itself as "a school of the future," Belle Valley is a neighborhood elementary school derived from the application of Quality principles. As a result of an educational partnership with Apple Computer, Inc., the school is a phenomenon of technology. Over 400 Macintosh computers are being used in classrooms by students and teachers, in the library/media center, and in the administrative offices, to ensure that technology is fully integrated into all students' learning processes.

The current Belle Valley School replaced an old six-room school building. Rather than follow previous procedures for planning a new school, the district engaged in consensus building to design this school. A planning team comprised of administrators, teachers, parents, nonteaching staff, and other com-

munity members met with an outside facilities planner for over
a year to talk about the way they wanted their school to look and
to work. The key Quality tool that transformed the team's ideas
into practice was the development of the "education specifications," which outlined the "family and community" theme of the
school, the general and specific facility implications reflected by
the educational program needs, and access to the community in
general.

"We met in large groups, then small groups to work out
specific areas such as the futures center, music, PE. Ideas would
build on one another, because we all had an idea of how it
should be," explains Kathleen Bukowski, supervisor of elementary education, who led the Belle Valley planning team. "We had
to keep reminding the architect that we were *his* customers,
because he had never worked like this before. Eventually, he
understood what we were doing and was calling us to ask for our
opinions. It's all worked out for the best. And we can't blame
him for any mistakes—and there aren't many. We made the
decisions, so we're responsible. It was a wonderful quality
process in action." After two years, the team arrived at a plan
that was pleasing to all. The new Belle Valley School building is
arranged by grade-level "houses," each designed to encourage a
flexible environment for teachers and students. Since the district was launching cooperative learning in its operations, the
teachers (all of whom applied to teach in the school) work in
teams, which are facilitated by the flexible arrangement of the
classrooms. Some other Belle Valley features worth noting are
the following:

- There are four classrooms for each grade, situated around
  a "family room." In each classroom, the wall that faces the
  "family room" is glass. The walls between the classrooms are
  movable, so the classrooms can be separate or opened to
  one another.
- Superintendent Agnew believes that the principal as a
  Quality agent should be based as close to the instructional
  areas as possible. Barbara Maasz is the Belle Valley School
  principal, and she was an active participant on the planning
  team. She requested that her office be placed in the center

of the building and that the walls be glass. That way, she can see what is going on outside her office, and, more important, others can see what is going on inside her office.

- The studio is a flex room that can serve as a television studio and can also be used for large-group activities. It is constructed like an auditorium—that is, tiered down toward a stage—but there are no chairs. The team decided that young children are not comfortable in regulation auditorium chairs. Kids being kids, they would rather sit on the floor, stretch out, and move around. So the tiers were carpeted, which eliminated the chairs and, as a side benefit for being customer focused, saved money.

Other design features are consistent with one planning team goal—to make the new Belle Valley have the "old-time" feeling of the neighborhood school it replaced. At the same time, it meets the other goals of preparing students for the challenges of change and helping teachers to better understand and utilize computer technology.

An additional note: Since our visit, Millcreek opened a new middle school in September 1993. Everyone was so delighted with Belle Valley that the district used the same technique to plan this new school—with one important difference. It took two years to plan Belle Valley; it took seven months to plan the new middle school.

Human Resource Development and Management

Baldrige definition: The *Human Resource Planning and Development* Category examines the key elements of how the work force is enabled to develop its full potential to pursue the organization's quality and operational performance objectives. Also examined are the organization's efforts to build and maintain an environment for quality excellence conducive to full participation and personal and organizational growth.

Superintendent of Rappahannock County Public Schools David Gangel commented: "The biggest part is human. Skills can be learned, but the attitudes are harder to change."

Human Resource Planning and Management

For the most part, the education sites were working to ensure that their overall human resource development and management plans and practices supported their organizations' Quality and performance plans. In matters ranging from hiring to staff development to labor-management cooperation, decision makers were applying the principles of Quality. For example, as Rappahannock County planned its venture into Quality under the auspices of a Commonwealth of Virginia grant, Superintendent David Gangel included representatives from the administration as well as teaching and noninstructional staff in the initial training offered by Xerox. Now that Quality has become ingrained throughout the school district, part of the process for hiring new staff includes an assessment of whether they will fit into the district's Quality culture. Interview questions are asked that will ascertain such things as their willingness to work in teams and their propensity to learn the problem-solving processes. "Those who say things like 'I don't have the time for that' are simply not hired," explains Gangel.

Student and Employee Involvement

Many of the sites shared a goal of finding ways for all students and employees to contribute effectively to meet the Quality objectives. Utilizing people's expertise to bolster the collaborative effort with useful information engaged the entire education community in key decision making. In Millcreek Township, the entire district worked to meet the criteria specified by the Erie Excellence Award. At Mt. Edgecumbe High School, students as sophisticated developers, users, and ultimately teachers of the school's computer software assisted the administrators and teachers as they advanced their Quality processes.

Training

"Every employee is important to a Quality organization," was a frequently repeated message in all eleven sites. But for employees to contribute to organizational success, they must have training in the necessary skills. Particularly in education, where the customary behavior is to close the classroom door and do things the same way year after year, the concepts of Quality have to be learned and opportunities for practice have to be structured.

For example, data-driven decision making is one of the tenets of Quality. An educator's typical training, however, excludes statistics and the application of any kind of deductive reasoning for problem solving. As Gail Hubbard, Prince William County Gifted Program supervisor, says, "When educators solve problems, they do so without analysis. They don't use facts for analytical processes." Yet after exposure to training in simple statistical tools, school-based problem-solving teams can analyze data and suggest ways of accomplishing the following:

- Revising curriculum (Southwestern Wisconsin Quality Consortium)
- Reducing the number of student failures (Parkview School District and George Westinghouse VTHS)
- Raising ACT scores (School District of Beloit Turner)
- Eliminating bus discipline problems (Rappahannock County Public Schools)
- Improving the hiring and selection process (Brodhead School District)
- Developing governance structures for site-based management teams (Brodhead School District)

Students, too, can be trained to use the tools to monitor their own academic progress (Mt. Edgecumbe High School and Parkview School District).

There is no one way to provide training. Methods in our sites ranged from a structured, business-based model to an ad hoc system, where training was made available to whomever showed interest. The two Northern Virginia school districts, Rappahannock and Prince William Counties, and the Vermont Department of Education used the Xerox method. Selected staff from these education sites attended Xerox's *Leadership Through Quality* training and worked with Xerox staff. Very little of the business vocabulary was changed to accommodate education concepts or language; instead, the training participants did the necessary translation as they went along. Participants spent four days in exercises designed to teach them the Xerox process skills—interactive skills, meeting skills, and the problem-solving processes. For some, working in teams to analyze and solve problems using facts was an entirely new experience. Fred Malnichak, a principal who attended the Xerox training, describes the four-day session: "It was the best thing. The natural marriage between site-based management and Quality was obvious. Quality is the vehicle for us to become better decision makers."

Responses to the "strictly business" training were mixed. A few educators found it disconcerting and were put off by the business terminology. But most found the entire training program, including the vocabulary and the exercises, to be completely applicable once they had the opportunity to work with the materials. Advises David Gangel: "Language doesn't have to be a problem. Just talk more about what it can do, and don't get caught up in what it's called."

Who Gets Trained? All of the education sites underwent some form of training, although *who* was offered the training differed. In every site, the superintendent was among the first to get trained, but others in the initial training group varied. Ed Kelly, superintendent of Prince William County Public Schools, was joined by key central office staff, plus the principal and lead teacher in each of the district's three TQM pilot schools. Their plan is to eventually train all 7,500 of the Prince William County staff over the next three to four years, after training in-house staff to provide a Xerox-based training program.

Following are ways in which some of the other education sites offered training to varied members of the staff and student bodies:

- In Rappahannock County, training was given to teaching and nonteaching staff simultaneously, allowing cross-functional teams to work together from the start.
- Franklin Schargel, George Westinghouse VTHS assistant principal, arranged formal Quality training for his principal, Lewis Rappaport, and himself. He contacted local businesses, which then allowed the two high school administrators to attend their training. Rappaport and Schargel arranged for subsequent training by other private companies for staff, parents, and students. They held a lottery to see who would attend an IBM-sponsored training weekend. Students, parents, teachers, administrators, and nonteaching staff, including the head security guard, spent two days at IBM's Palisades training center. Others in the school have requested that they be able to attend the next training session. "We've had wonderful cooperation from businesses," explains Schargel. "Once they understand what we are trying to do, they are very generous about helping us to bring Quality to Westinghouse."
- David Langford, Mt. Edgecumbe High School teacher, was exposed to TQM through an Arizona colleague. He attempted to bring it to his own high school in Alaska but initially was unable to engage his superintendent or other staff. He decided to learn as much as he could on his own, while introducing it to his students. It was not until after he and his students became more proficient that he again tried to introduce it to the whole school. This time, the students did the presentation, which captivated the rest of the school, the staff, and the superintendent, Larrae Rocheleau. Rocheleau described their presentation in superlatives. "I've never seen kids so turned on by what they were doing," he said. "I knew that we had to get into this in a big way." Following the students' presentation, training was introduced to most staff (teaching and nonteaching) and to many of the students.
- The Erie Excellence Council has expanded its North Coast Quality Week activities to include a North Coast Education Day. In 1992 and 1993, teachers from the seventeen–school

district region attended sessions with consultants in Quality and met with teachers from throughout the region to learn about and practice Quality.

How Is Training Offered?   Once again, there were many variations on this theme. For example, as a member of the National Center on Education and the Economy's Alliance for Restructuring, the Vermont Department of Education has had assistance in its move to Quality. Norm Deets, an executive on loan from Xerox to the National Center on Education and the Economy, met regularly with a transition team to assist team members in their strategic planning and to provide some training himself. Additional training has been offered by another Xerox-trained consultant. The department has been training in Xerox's *Leadership Through Quality*, which is being offered currently to cross-functional teams. The entire department has been trained by in-house trainers. In addition, the department has provided Quality training to a team from the state's social services agency. The two state departments are engaged already in interagency agreements pertaining to integrated services for Vermont's young people. They are confident that they will all benefit greatly from their use of Quality tools for joint problem solving.

To take another example, Prince William County selected three pilot schools to receive training from Xerox. The principal and a lead teacher attended training along with the superintendent and key members of his staff. Training for additional staff in the pilot schools has been a combination of Xerox training (until those funds were depleted) and in-house training. The district goal is to train all employees over the next three to four years.

The Southwestern Wisconsin Quality Consortium has also used a combination of training opportunities. They pooled their resources to hire two consultants—one for Quality and the other for outcome-based education. TQM techniques have been modeled and used as staffs from the combined districts have formed cross-functional teams to revise their curriculum. Each of the member districts has also established Curriculum Coordinating Councils (CCCs), and these councils have received training from their shared consultant. Additionally, the superintendents have participated in training offered by groups such as the American Association of School Administrators and specialized Quality organizations.

Millcreek Township has been somewhat ad hoc in its approach to training, encouraging Quality to spread throughout the district. Administrators have provided formal training to some staff using outside consultants, and they have offered voluntary courses as a part of their menu of required in-service training. The Form Cutters received "just-in-time" training and some printed materials from Verel Salmon as they were going through their exercise on the travel request form. Openings in local corporate training are made available to staff on a first-come, first-served basis.

Most of the education sites have incorporated student and employee education and training into their operations:

- Parkview has created fifty-seven hours of staff development for each teacher. Teachers attend one-half day per month all year.
- Training in the use of Quality tools involved the entire Brodhead support staff, who identified quality indicators and desired outcomes for each individual employment classification. The results became an integral part of each employee's job description.
- At Mt. Edgecumbe, the superintendent, principals, and teachers were initially given fifteen hours of intensive training and discussion time during the first year. At the end of the training process, everyone voted whether or not they wanted to continue, and the vote was unanimous to adopt the new philosophy. Although there were some who wanted to retract their vote during the following year, TQM became the school's stated position by the end of the second year. Education and training needs were addressed during the second year, when administrators created a schedule that would provide two ninety-minute training/planning/problem-solving sessions per week for both students and staff.
- Students at Mt. Edgecumbe are trained in the quality principles and tools. A matrix, *Understanding Quality Resource/*

Competency Matrix, has been developed for students to self-assess and track their progress on the competencies.

- In Millcreek, a course in TQM is now a requirement for students' graduation. The district created the course three years ago, and it is now a component of the high school economics class. Many students have the opportunity to use their Quality skills as they participate in their respective schools' companies.

Recognition

Regardless of how self-motivated and self-directed, most people enjoy receiving sincere praise from their co-workers, supervisors, and customers. Quality organizations realize how important recognition and celebration are to everyone's morale and well-being and ensure there are opportunities for both. This reinforces the notion that everyone is important to the success and continuous improvement of the organization. Recognition ranges from huge competitions à la Xerox and Motorola, to a note or a memo. Chuck Melvin, superintendent of the School District of Beloit Turner, tries to acknowledge staff efforts as often and in as many ways as he can. Typical is the closing to a memo addressed to his transportation problem-solving team: "Again, thank you for your assistance as we continue to investigate how every part of the school system can do its job better."

Celebrations

Most people also like to celebrate achievements. As an example, George Westinghouse VTHS values its staff and makes it a point to communicate that message as often as possible. The school has instituted an "employee of the month" program. The first winner was one of their maintenance workers. The name of the designated employee is announced over the school's public address system and a small cash award, a plaque, and a congratulatory letter are presented at a faculty conference. In truth, the money is the least important aspect of the recognition ritual. When the staff members became aware that cash might no longer be available for the award, they wanted the program to continue regardless, noting that the greatest satisfaction came from receiving recognition at the faculty conference and having their peers acknowledge their accomplishment.

George Westinghouse also listened to parents. They wanted a gathering to reinforce the importance of family involvement in an urban environment that constantly negated that notion. The PTA planned a Family Night, where families brought a variety of ethnic foods to the school cafeteria. Almost all staff and many families and students attended. The gathering was judged to be a success by all who came, and the PTA decided to make it an annual event.

Other approaches are also possible. Each organization within the Millcreek Township School District actively supports and reinforces employees who are involved in and contribute to Quality improvement efforts. Recognition includes daily audio or video announcements acknowledging student and staff accomplishments, a school district employee-of-the-month award, student "attendance counts" awards, a perfect attendance dinner and awards, a computer loan/purchase program, PTA and district operation appreciation programs, and opportunities for administrators to carry out an approved improvement project beyond the scope of their regular duties in a new performance pay plan (Millcreek's application for the Erie Excellence Council's Quality Award).

Management of Process Quality

Baldrige definition: The *Management of Process Quality* Category examines the systematic processes the organization uses to pursue ever-higher quality and organizational operational performance. Examined are the key elements of process management, including research and development, design, management of process quality for all work units and suppliers, systematic quality improvement, and quality assessment.

According to the Continuous Improvement Plan of the Rappahannock County Public Schools: "In general, the Quality

Improvement Plan (QIP) is the tool used to develop new processes. Within the school system, the major area for new service development is curriculum development."

The education sites we visited have been changing their methods for designing, monitoring, and assessing all of their "business"—curriculum, activities, learning processes, noninstructional processes—since they began to practice Quality. They have kept their collective eyes on using data to solve problems and make decisions, as well as to try to continuously improve their work processes. They have attempted to be more inclusive when it comes to making decisions by forming teams that include parents and other community members, in addition to teaching and nonteaching personnel. Yet all acknowledge that they are still in the "learner" phase; they know it will take them time to get to the point where this is the way they do their business.

Developing Structures to Align Goals Within the Education Organization

Aligning the goals for classrooms, school buildings, districts, and state and federal governments is a balancing act requiring frequent and articulate communication of goals and practices. Following are examples of structures put in place to ensure that alignment occurs.

Southwestern Wisconsin Quality Consortium. The consortium played a significant role in the statewide adoption of outcome-based education. Representing the group of five school districts, Parkview School District superintendent Dave Romstad "shadowed" a one-year governor's commission charged with making recommendations for new designs in education. Romstad played the same role as the state legislature held its hearings on education restructuring in general and outcome-based education specifically.

With both groups, Romstad was able to describe the actions taken by the consortium districts to make outcome-based education work, and the successes they were seeing. "It was important," Romstad says, "for both statewide groups to understand that we were already having some success doing what they were debating. We needed their support, and they needed us as an example of how it could work. It was symbiosis at work." The legislation was passed. Romstad describes the state support as very helpful in convincing the "resisters" in the consortium, too. He says, "We could truthfully tell them that the State is going ahead with this, so we may as well be ahead of the curve." It paid off. Romstad describes a high school teacher who began the school year by telling him, "Dr. Romstad, you know I've been a doubter of all this from the beginning. But you were right. It works. And I'm so glad we're doing it before the State tells us we have to."

Mt. Edgecumbe High School. In order to encourage his students to become managers of their own Quality process, David Langford developed and wrote a manual for Mt. Edgecumbe High School students that provided them with forms for monitoring their own work processes. He taught both teachers and students statistical graphing techniques such as run charts, histograms, Pareto charts, and control charts and helped to get people in the habit of recording data. As a result, students and teachers began to understand the concepts of variation, process, monitoring data, inspection, and statistical graphing and became comfortable in using this information to make decisions for themselves that were aligned with Mt. Edgecumbe's mission and goals.

The Mt. Edgecumbe students monitored their various classes and plotted how much time was spent in lectures, how much on hands-on learning. They used sampling techniques and found only ten minutes of hands-on work in a fifty-minute lecture. Once teachers realized what was actually happening, they began to provide shorter lectures and more hands-on work. They also modified class schedules from seven fifty-minute periods to four ninety-minute periods. In essence, the students at Mt. Edgecumbe were focused on improving their learning. They understood the necessity of becoming lifelong learners and realized how Quality could help them to reach that goal by making them managers of their own Quality processes.

Quality and Operational Results

Baldrige definition: The *Quality and Operational Results* Category examines the organization's quality levels and improvement trends in quality, organization operational performance, and supplier quality. Also examined are current quality and operational performance levels relative to those of competitors.

Larrae Rocheleau, former Superintendent, Mt. Edgecumbe High School, observed: "The ultimate result is if the school is doing its job, the kids will develop a 'yearning for learning.'"

This criterion looks at the actual results demonstrated by the education sites in all areas—from learning processes to labor-management negotiations to food service activities. That is, what has *really* happened since the Quality processes were put in place? What has changed? What do the changes look like? How have results compared to original goals? The following sections describe solutions to educational problems that were reached by applying Quality tools.

Improving Student Performance

Using the Quality approach, schools and school districts have been able to dramatically improve student performance.

George Westinghouse VTHS. The school had a serious problem: 151 students were failing *every* course. The staff brainstormed and decided to bring parents into their discussions and decisions. They decided to have the school, the parents, and each student sign a contract and then customize the school program to meet the student's needs. They were able to reduce the total failures to eleven students—still not perfect, but a decided improvement. They repeated the process the following year, making every effort to get the students to class and to succeed. For example, they made adjustments to some class schedules and started the day later for some to ensure student attendance.

Parkview and Brodhead School Districts. These two Wisconsin school districts have compiled some impressive results. Only a few years ago, the statistics on student performance at Parkview were alarming. In 1987–88 there was a 29 percent failure rate (F in at least one course), as well as low standardized test scores, especially in the tenth grade. But in 1989–90, the failure rate declined by over 60 percent, the honor roll membership increased by 50 percent, and the number of students attending postsecondary institutions increased from 60 to 84 percent. In 1990–91, the failure rate declined 68 percent; in 1991–92, it declined 73 percent.

In the Brodhead School District, there were 1,049 student discipline referrals in 1988–89. But in 1990–91, the number declined to only 481. In addition, scores on the Stanford achievement tests rose 33 percent in fourth-grade mathematics, 89 percent of third-grade students exceeded the state average in reading, participation in extracurricular activities increased 104 percent, and the number of students taking Advanced Placement tests for college credit rose 600 percent. In 1991–92, 90 percent of students went on to post–high school education or training opportunities.

Reducing Cycle Time in Facilitating Contract Negotiations

The School District of Beloit Turner made dramatic changes in its processes when it came time to negotiate the 1992–94 teachers' contract. The sessions began with a "problems identification" meeting, using Quality tools to keep the meeting positive, on time, and on point. At the end of each subsequent meeting, negotiators discussed the agenda for the following meeting and added new items with mutual consent. Graphing their findings on Pareto charts, they identified five areas where there was the most consensus as to need: (1) responsibility, (2) incentives, (3) fragmented attendance, (4) training, and (5) extended contract. This kind of structure and focus made the negotiations go much more smoothly and positively.

Implementing Noninstructional Improvements

Quality has been used to implement noninstructional improvements at various education sites.

Parkview School District. The district's food service workers have not only moved their budget from the red to the black but have turned a $60,000 profit. Initially, staff worked with Dave Romstad, the superintendent, but quickly struck out on their own. According to Romstad: "I talked to them about employee empowerment, setting goals, and working in teams. They took it from there. And they haven't stopped." By focusing on their customers' needs, the food service workers expanded the à la carte menu, spent more time developing their menu with staff and students, and sponsored holiday buffet feasts. The student council has assisted them in measuring their progress by surveying the students' responses to the changes.

Millcreek Township School District. The school district administrators studied support services and decided they could save money if they bid some of these services—transportation and maintenance management—to outside suppliers. Part of the process included the contractors' commitment to Quality, which had become one of Millcreek's selection criteria. They ultimately selected Servicemaster to oversee the maintenance contract and Ryder Bus Company for their transportation needs. Millcreek awarded Ryder the contract even though the bus company was not the lowest bidder. It was, however, committed to TQM. Since selecting Ryder, Millcreek has saved hundreds of thousands of dollars in its transportation and maintenance costs, which has been used for capital improvements.

Customer Focus and Satisfaction

> Baldrige definition: The *Customer Focus and Satisfaction* Category examines the organization's relationships with customers and its knowledge of customer requirements and of the key quality factors that drive marketplace competitiveness. Also examined are the organization's methods to determine customer satisfaction, current trends and levels of customer satisfaction and retention, and these results relative to competitors.

As Parkview School District principal Don Albrecht put it: "The student is customer—they're the reason we're here."

We asked people in both the education and private sectors the following question: "What is your personal definition of Quality?" Almost everyone mentioned customer satisfaction.

Sometimes it was in the context of doing things right the first time to please the customer; sometimes it was based on problem solving in anticipation of customer needs. Leadership, vision, and culture were also included in their definitions, but more often than not, customer satisfaction was most significant to their understanding and practice of Quality.

In addition, all of the organizations we visited went out of their way to solicit feedback in order to ensure that they were satisfying their customers. Depending on one's job, there were different customers. This resulted in many different measures of customer satisfaction. For example, at Mt. Edgecumbe High School, the "student-as-customer" theme is articulated consistently. Individual teachers survey students—formally and informally—to ensure that the students are understanding and applying what they are learning. The school surveys its students following their graduation, benchmarking them against other high school graduates. It also attempts to keep in contact with the parents, no mean feat when one realizes that Mt. Edgecumbe draws students from all over the State of Alaska.

In Rappahannock County, annual customer surveys are sent to staff and parents at the beginning and end of the school year. Data have been solicited from teachers about cooperative learning. And parent satisfaction with the district's various programs—communication with teachers and administration, discipline, safety, and transportation—has been measured. Because continuous improvement is such an important aspect of Rappahannock's strategic plan, the survey results form the basis for problem-solving teams and revised programs and curriculum.

Millcreek surveys colleges and businesses to ensure that their graduates are meeting the expectations of this set of customers. They also survey students to ensure that the product—student learning—has served them well. The collected data go back to academic teams to be integrated in curriculum changes.

Millcreek also engaged its internal and external customers—school staff and community members—in an exercise to articulate their current and future expectations. With support from futurist Joel Barker, they developed a Vision Statement, which serves as a reference tool for continuous improvement.

The Vision Statement is a fictionalized account of a family and their three children, ages three, twelve, and eighteen years old, respectively, who are Millcreek students in the year 2000. It describes such things as the children's school experiences, the courses they take, the staff's methods of teaching, the technology they use, and the organization of their schools and the community. Millcreek has found that by looking ahead with the people who will be served, they are more likely to serve their needs.

To consider a final example, George Westinghouse VTHS has been surveying parents to assess their customer satisfaction for the past three years. Suggestions from parents have influenced such things as the content of PTA meetings and services that are being offered to students. As a result, parent interest has been aroused—that is, membership in the PTA has risen and regular attendance at meetings has increased. Staff at the high school are continuing to meet and exceed the needs of this group.

All education sites concurred that how the data are used is just as important as collecting the data. And all the sites are trying to use their data to measure progress and improve processes and programs.

Supplier Quality: Managing Customer Demands

Realizing that the state legislature was one of its key external customers, the Vermont Department of Education wanted to be responsive. At the same time, the department wanted the lawmakers to be able to assess the costs of their requests. A problem-solving exercise inside the department resulted in processing requests from the legislature differently to (1) meet the needs of the customer and (2) make the customer aware of the quantity and quality of time devoted to responding to requests. For example, when a request for information regarding the number of students in tech-prep was made, the education specialist asked the lawmaker, "What exactly do you want?" before beginning the research. When the staff person submitted the report, the number of hours and dollars spent in responding to the request was printed on the cover. This practice is being put into place for all legislative and executive requests for information.

The Ultimate Customer Satisfaction

Having the "voice of the customer" direct work-process improve-ments provides as much opportunity for restructuring education as it does for restructuring private industry. Lisa Marie Polk, a stu-dent at Mt. Edgecumbe, summed up the ultimate customer's sat-isfaction this way: "The benefit of all this," concludes Polk about using Quality, "is that it is helping us to visualize adulthood."

An Additional Word About the Baldrige Criteria

Increasing numbers of educators are interested in using the Baldrige (or similar Quality) Criteria as a self-assessment tool that focuses their organizations on student and system perfor-mance. By concentrating on learning goals for students, for example, the self-assessment process could help educators raise key organizational questions in redesigning school systems around the needs of children, rather than adults. Using the Baldrige Criteria to evaluate educational operations also pro-vides a means for business leaders to support the efforts of edu-cators in building internal capacity to make continuous improvements. The Criteria would help educators examine and improve all—not just a few—of their work processes concur-rently. The "whole" would become greater, yielding better results, than the sum of the pieces. The use of the Baldrige Cri-teria, customized for education organizations, could reinforce reform efforts nationwide in the following ways.

Help Education Systems Articulate Their Goal

In industry, the goal of the Baldrige Criteria is to "project key requirements for delivering ever-improving value to customers while at the same time maximizing the overall effectiveness and productivity of the delivering organization." Similarly in educa-tion, the goal could assist educators to "project their key requirements for delivering ever-improving value—*learning*—to *students and their primary 'customers'* (for example, parents, higher education, and employers) while maximizing the overall effectiveness and productivity of *school systems.*"

Guide Local Self-Assessment Efforts

Collectively, the seven Baldrige Criteria serve as an important organization resource. They provide an organizational framework to take stock of and realign management processes to focus on results, a means to reassess progress on an ongoing basis so that improvements can be implemented and evaluated over time, and a common language and "decision-making lens" across different types of organizations so they can work together in making improvements.

Help Educators Evaluate Their Progress

Assessing themselves on the Baldrige Award Criteria compels organizations to come to terms with three key evaluation issues:

- The *approaches* they use in addressing each piece of the system framework
- The extent to which they *deploy* (implement) such approaches throughout the organization
- The *results* they achieve

Underscore the Benefits of Using Quality Practices

Far more than serving as the basis for selecting National Quality Award recipients from industry each year, the Baldrige Criteria fulfill other important purposes, which could also be extended to education. They:

- Raise Quality performance standards and expectations in organizations across the country
- Serve as a working tool for organizations to identify their planning, training, and assessment needs
- Facilitate communication among and within organizations based on a common understanding of Quality
- Provide the means for organizations to receive feedback on making improvements

A growing number of states and communities are sponsoring their own Quality awards. Based largely on the multiple purposes and impact of the Baldrige Award, these initiatives could also help spur adoption of Quality practices in education and other public sector organizations.

Chapter 6

The Education System
An Oxymoron?

One objective of Chapter Six is to underscore the parallels between business and education organizations in applying Quality. And there are many, as previous chapters illustrate. A second, more compelling objective is to reflect on the differences—the added perils in education—which present significant challenges for educators committed to implementing TQM.

The Parallels

What began as a business transformation strategy—Total Quality Management—is being customized for and applied successfully in education. Anecdotes and examples abound throughout this book as prima facie evidence of the relevance of TQM to an education setting. To recap, the key similarities between education and business in using Quality include a focus on the customer; committed, involved leadership; a trusting, supportive culture; the commitment and resources to provide training at all organizational levels; and the use of new skills and tools to make key decisions. The most fundamental parallel between business and education leaders using Quality practices and tools is their common reference point—a shared vision of a postindustrial learning environment, both in school and at work—and what they have done about it.

Like successful businesspeople, educators from the sites we visited are setting high standards that define what students need to know and be able to do. And they are restructuring their work processes in order to meet more rigorous standards. These educators are using Quality practices and tools to address common issues. They are identifying the root cause of existing barriers and devising strategies to remove them. And they are reducing cycle time and eliminating steps in work processes not value added to serving their students. These educators are attempting to design Quality into the system at the front end so that their students have the ability and the will to improve their own learning capacity continuously, now and into the future— as part of learning communities and as lifelong learners. Such is the promise, ultimately, that TQM holds for education.

Many other educators are not so fortunate or forward thinking. The assembly-line industrial model, long since abandoned by successful companies, still characterizes most education settings. "Education places children on a conveyor belt at age six," notes Ted Sanders, Ohio superintendent of public instruction. "When many of the 'products' are found to be defective, they are simply cast off. Moreover, there is little concern for the wide variance in the final product."

Companies that abandoned the industrial model—and mindset—stress Quality over pushing products out the door at any cost and in whatever shape. "Getting it right the first time," they discovered, is smart business, not only because it satisfies customers and keeps them coming back, but because it costs less. Educators confront a similar challenge and opportunity. Assembly-line education no longer works, because too many children are falling off the conveyor belt, literally, by dropping out of school or graduating without knowing what they need to know.

Reducing cycle time and eliminating defects in business and ensuring that "all kids can learn" in education are parallel goals. Like business, education will achieve *Six Sigma* only when all students graduate on time and when their diplomas mean something. To be able to serve all children well, education needs to develop the capacity to vary its instructional processes in order to ensure high performance in every child, across the board. What it will take to make this happen differs for each child and in each community. "There must be unity of purpose but not unity of method," observes Sanders. In other words, all children can learn *and will*, but not in the same way.

The Perils: Additional Challenges in Education

Educators are demonstrating by "doing it" that Quality works in their organizations, much as it does in business. That is the good news. The bad news, based on the perceptions of educators from these sites as well as our own experiences in working with numerous other education sites and businesses, is a "yes, but . . ."

The additional hurdles in applying TQM in education include the following:

- A disconnected system—that is, how can there be *systemic* reform when the nature and boundaries of *the system* cannot be assumed?
- A more complicated leadership structure and set of stakeholders
- Undefined work processes
- Complex customer-supplier relationships
- Limited, unfocused training resources and opportunities
- Severe time constraints
- A built-in bias in favor of the short term
- A temptation, without setting ambitious goals and measuring progress, for TQM to become an end in itself

Redesigning the System

Education has been in the throes of major change for over a decade. What prompted the flurry of education reform activity in the early 1980s was a recognized need to focus on results. *A Nation at Risk* and other influential reports claimed the country's attention by pointing out that, for too long, education policy and funding decisions had centered on providing inputs without regard to outcomes and that school districts were not connected, in any strategic sense, to inputs or outcomes. The reports viewed the organization of a school district negatively as "the black box" or worse yet, "the bureaucracy." Process became "the black hole," perceived as delaying or even preventing progress. And it often did. Warned of this "rising tide of mediocrity," state after state enacted a breakwall of top-down reforms.

Today, that breakwall is coming down. Having learned that mandates can require action but not improvement, increasing numbers of states and districts are transferring to individual schools the authority for key decisions—their rationale being that those closest to the customers are best positioned to understand and meet their needs. Unfortunately, in many cases, the empowerment stops with the rhetoric. The foundation and connectors that link schools to the rest of the system are weak or absent. What is missing, in essence, is the organizational capacity in education to connect *intended* outcomes with the *actual* work processes that could produce them. The challenge of implementing Quality in the education *system*, then, is not merely to adopt new operating practices but to create the organizational infrastructure that supports the new practices. This is not meant to imply that companies can control all the inputs into their system. But successful companies have figured out ways to manage such inputs as new tax policies, trade agreements, and environmental regulations so they do not become electrons and neutrons bouncing around inside their organizations but rather policies translated eventually into company practice.

Conversely, in education, it is not always clear when a decision is a decision. Because there is no connection between most inputs and work processes, many people within education organizations have to sign off on decisions before action can proceed. Some decisions, once approved, may still be ignored or go unfulfilled because support, incentive, and accountability mechanisms are not factored in. With this organizational labyrinth as a backdrop, it is not surprising that educators who implement TQM favor a voluntary participation model. They have figured out that "legislating" Quality probably would not work anyway.

There are other important organizational differences between education and business that contribute to education's inability to act systemically. For one, companies can rely on certain "givens" where education organizations cannot. Organizational boundaries in the private sector are such a given. Inside are all the people who do the work. Outside are suppliers at one end and customers at the other. Although individual responsibilities in Quality settings are merging into a more seamless system, their separate identities—as suppliers, workers, or customers—remain easily discernible.

The organizational boundaries, roles, and relationships are not nearly as delineated in education, given the multitiered governance structure and impact of policymakers and external constituencies on the decisions. Numerous institutions, from the Congress to the classroom and from school districts laterally to social service agencies, juvenile probation, and employment and training offices in the greater community, have the ability to drive educational activity. And in the process, they often drive each other away. All too frequently, the pieces of the education system emphasize their differences, their turf, as the rationale for not trying to reach common ground. Successful companies, by contrast, seek out the connectors, so they can build on their common ground to address and resolve their differences.

Thus, before we can "fix" the education system, we first must raise a more compelling question: What is "the education system"? In other words, is the education system an oxymoron? If not, how do we bring together the "black boxes" and "black holes" at the federal, state, community, district, and school levels—a loosely coupled system, if you will—to form a functional entity? There needs to be a way to connect the dots.

Reconnecting Humpty Dumpty

The source of authority in education is fractured and no one has yet figured out a good way to put Humpty Dumpty back together. Whereas leadership practices in business can be exercised unilaterally, they rarely are in education. Because power is shared, education decisions need to be consensus driven and collaborative. In addition, bad news in a public sector environment often is not forthcoming, and for understandable reasons. Bad news can be used to blame people rather than improve organizations. Consequently, sharing the results of a self-assessment becomes tricky, particularly for elected officials whose communities may kill the messengers by choosing not to reelect them. Not unlike coaches after a losing season, the same situation can endanger the contracts of school superintendents who share bad news with their potential messenger killers—boards of education. And such behavior often engenders a ripple effect, with superintendents beating up on principals, principals on teachers, and teachers on students and parents—a giant food chain of casting blame—the very antithesis of a Quality process. It's no one person's fault that Humpty Dumpty broke apart. But it's everyone's responsibility to put him back together again.

Governance and Leadership: A Distinction with a Difference

Boards of directors in the businesses we visited generally were not a factor in the company's decision to implement TQM. The directors viewed implementation as a management issue and the CEO's prerogative. They were supportive because TQM is customer focused but did not get involved in determining the day-to-day operations, which they correctly perceived as an administrative issue.

In education, the distinction between policymaking/oversight and operations is not nearly so discrete. As duly elected representatives of their communities, school boards have an obligation to make policy that represents community interests. Their success as board members and often their reelection depend on how effectively the district executes those policies. All too often, however, board members get immersed in daily school operations as well.

When it comes to Quality, school boards need to become involved, in order to enhance their ability to make good policy decisions. They also must become engaged as a preventive measure. Board members can terminate a carefully planned, long-term change process simply by firing the superintendent—an action that is becoming increasingly common in education. In contrast, board members in this study illustrate the constructive roles that boards can play in supporting Quality implementation. They can help spread the word in the community and support administrators who are making positive changes.

The nature of their obligation to customers is another fundamental distinction between corporate leadership and educational governance. For example, business leaders can decide to "fire" their customers, simply by choosing not to serve them. Companies that have sold off parts of their business, ceased production of unprofitable goods and services, or closed shop in certain markets have done just that. Such decisions, difficult as they are, at least have the comfort of being made in private.

In contrast, educators produce a public good, one they are constitutionally obligated to deliver to all who show up at the school house door. They cannot "cut their losses" by refusing to serve certain customers, which makes the task of educating all children successfully all the more challenging. And educators must deliver the goods out in the open, within the tangled context of complicated, frequently contradictory federal and state policies. This observation should not be misconstrued as an argument favoring limiting public access to education or promoting closed-door meetings. Rather, it simply acknowledges the relative latitude of exercising leadership in the private sector when compared to governing in education.

Work Processes: Will We Know Them When We See Them?

At the core of TQM is defining, tracking, and improving work processes—that is, understanding the ways in which people are organized to work and do their work—so as to obtain favorable results.

One of the surprises in conducting this study was discovering the extent to which results-oriented, bottom-line businesses emphasize the soft, people-oriented side of TQM. (It should be reassuring for some educators who may think otherwise to learn that the private sector has a human side after all.) On further reflection, business's emphasis on enhancing the human relations skills of their entire workforce is not at all surprising. It is strategic. Prior to implementing TQM, successful companies (in contrast to education) already had clearly defined work processes in place. And they recognized up front the need to align work processes with their organizational culture. Therefore, in implementing Quality, the challenge for these companies was (and continues to be as the companies drive down decision-making authority) figuring out ways to enhance their people's ability to work together collaboratively and cross-functionally.

It bears repeating that the concept of work processes is relatively new in education. Obviously, decisions get made and work gets done, but there is no method to the madness, no recognized process that frames work. And for a very simple reason: Most educators were not trained to view what they do in a collective context. Instead, work is defined in the context of one's *job* (teacher, principal, superintendent) or one's *professional field* (counseling, curriculum development, special education), rather than being connected by a *process* to the work of others whose *collective* purpose is to meet customer needs. Yet the demands on educators have changed. It is important but no longer sufficient for them to become effective instructional leaders. Educators also must be prepared in college to view their roles and responsibilities within a larger organizational framework. Thus, in designing successful Quality implementation strategies, education leaders confront two significant challenges that many companies do not. They must build for their people an understanding of individual jobs and professional expertise as the sum total of connected work processes with a customer at the end of the process. And they must alter the organizational culture to support people working together.

Maintaining a collaborative work environment often is challenging under the best of circumstances. It is particularly challenging in education, given the built-in instability inside school systems. School boards are elected and subject to frequent turnover. Students are short-termers by definition. The whole point of school is to have them graduate. Consequently, for Quality to transform the learning enterprise, change efforts must appeal to and encompass the mainstay and most stable elements inside schools: teachers. For example, teachers must be trained and afforded opportunities to work collaboratively. How else can they be expected to assess the needs of their individual students within the context of a thirteen- to fourteen-year learning cycle? And teachers must be prepared to "translate" these needs of their students in ways that enable administrators responsible for instructional and noninstructional processes to provide support to them.

The Voice of the Customer: Choir or Mob?

TQM begins and ends with the voice of the customer. In successful companies, the voices may be tenor, alto, and soprano (segmented markets) but ultimately, they blend harmoniously in the choir. In education, the voice of the customer is more likely to come across as noise or, in worst-case scenarios, rabble from an angry mob.

Most of the sites we visited had no trouble accepting the musical score of Quality, *the business terminology*. School administrators, in particular, had reached a comfortable accommodation with the business language and problem-solving exercises, often preferring them to training materials customized for an education audience by some of the companies. In adapting the language of Quality to education, school leaders simply may need the opportunity to resolve for themselves the most appropriate terminology.

These positive notes, notwithstanding, it is the singers themselves—the *identity of the customers*—that is far more elusive in education than in business. And who the customer is, not how he/she is described, forms the crux of Quality. Although the concept of the *internal customer* is comparable in business and education, the real difference comes in process design. In education, the challenge is connecting internal customers to each other and, ultimately, to front-line workers—those internal customers who work directly with students. Nearly everyone in education says they are, thinks they are, and wants to be child focused. But the system (liberally defined) cannot tell them if they really are. Not all positions in education actually provide direct services to students, but many positions provide direct services to those who serve students. Thus, for education leaders the challenge is to create effective work processes where all of their people, working collaboratively and aware of everyone else's input, can add value that results in positive student outcomes.

When it comes to the identity of the *external customer*, education simply has more multiple personalities than does business. For example, the same individuals or institutions in education can be both suppliers and customers, depending on the product or transaction, as illustrated in Figure 6.1. The bottom line is that all key stakeholders—federal, state, and local policymakers; parents; business leaders; students; higher education; and communities and taxpayers—must be actively engaged with educators in *the same systemic change initiative* in support of life-long learning. The reality in many districts looks a lot different. School board members may be customer focused, but on different customers. Particularly in diverse communities, the sum total of members' independent actions may fail to represent—or even preclude the opportunity to represent—the customer requirements of the community as a whole.

Even concentrating organizational energies on the primary customer gets complicated. Educators in our study identified students as their *primary customers*. Unlike business, however, educators cannot focus exclusively on their primary customers to obtain their requirements. In the first place, students also have key customers they have to satisfy, such as their parents. And in the second place, particularly younger students (no matter how precocious) obviously will not be able to articulate all their requirements for a thorough and efficient education. But the opinions and advice of students should not be treated like afterthoughts in the dynamics of their own learning process, either.

Quite the opposite. As we learned from the students in our study, students who are given the opportunity can perform multiple customer roles. They can provide customer feedback, helping their teachers and administrators improve the delivery of education services. In noninstructional areas, students can offer feedback on such issues as the selection and quality of the cafeteria food or the range and quality of extracurricular activities. In more significant ways, students can offer feedback on the effectiveness of the instruction being delivered to them. They can let their teachers know: Was the information conveyed effectively? Do they understand their teacher's expectations?

Figure 6.1 Learning: Multiple Customer and Supplier Roles.

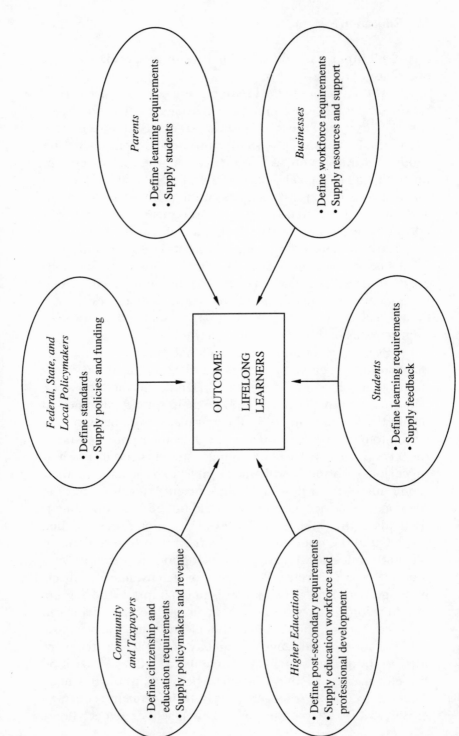

Parents
• Define learning requirements
• Supply students

Businesses
• Define workforce requirements
• Supply resources and support

Federal, State, and Local Policymakers
• Define standards
• Supply policies and funding

OUTCOME:
LIFELONG LEARNERS

Students
• Define learning requirements
• Supply feedback

Community and Taxpayers
• Define citizenship and education requirements
• Supply policymakers and revenue

Higher Education
• Define post-secondary requirements
• Supply education workforce and professional development

Source: National Alliance of Business.

Do they have adequate resources to complete the assignment? Does the assignment make sense and—for teachers who are real risk takers—is the assignment worth doing?

It should be acknowledged that many educators may find such changes threatening. As "the professionals," they may feel either that they have determined or should be able to determine where to go for the answers. The notion that students, let alone parents, can make a valuable contribution to the deliberations may threaten their sense of professional identity. But threatened or not, educators need to be key players (just not the only players) in redesigning learning processes. It also should be recognized that they stand to benefit greatly from the likely changes. Rather than having to wait for test scores or periodic performance assessments, educators could receive instant feedback that enhances their own continuous improvement efforts. And teachers will *know*, not just think they know, whether what they have taught has, in fact, been learned.

In addition to working on improving the system, students from our study demonstrated that young people can become actively engaged in improving their own performance. As managers of their own learning processes, students can be educated to use assessment data in tracking progress. As part of teams, they can learn at an early age to work collaboratively on solving problems. And the chance to receive ongoing feedback from teachers and peers can empower students, much like their teachers, to improve continuously. Unfortunately, more often than not, students are bystanders, not active participants, in their own learning process. Before they can assume responsibility for their own educational successes, a lot of adults must first engage them actively, both as customers and as co-workers.

Customer Needs: The Known, the Knowable, and the Unknown

Building an education system entirely around needs articulated by students and parents is likely to limit instruction in ways that do not serve students well in the future. Current perceptions of students and their parents may be based more on what is familiar and acceptable than on what is possible. For example, how many school boards and superintendents face community complacency (or even resistance) whenever they wish to make radical changes? The answer is "many," according to public opinion polls that verify the message "Education may be in trouble, but my school is fine" year after year. How many principals have seen parents push their kids, and students push themselves, to earn top grades that catch the eye of preeminent universities? Conversely, how many parents and students stress sports eligibility over academic achievement? And how many teachers have students in their classes who do not even try to learn, for fear of looking like "a geek" in the eyes of their peers? Sadly, students whose customer requirements are limited to earning top grades, maintaining sports eligibility, or impressing their friends may be precluding opportunities to have more compelling choices in the future.

Anticipating customer needs, beginning with but not limited to articulated needs, is a practice that the companies in this study engage in routinely. Customers did not know they would want and eventually need a copier before Xerox invented one. Drivers who talked to themselves were considered a little strange before Motorola car phones made such practice commonplace. And prior to Federal Express guarantees, many people with time-sensitive information simply sweated out the uncertainties of the U.S. mail or delivered it themselves.

Most loyal customers of copiers, car phones, and next-day delivery could not have anticipated their dependency on these products before they appeared on the market. But these products radically altered expectations and behavior. Limiting the definition of customer requirements to what customers *say* they need, based on existing knowledge, misses opportunities for breakthrough discoveries that may benefit customers in the future. Accordingly, the definition of "customer requirements" in education must extend beyond students, the primary customers, and even beyond their parents. The definition must encompass the requirements of *other customers of the primary customer*—demands from federal and state policymakers for an educated society; from business for a prepared workforce; and, not insignificantly, from educators whose professional judgments will determine what curricula and instructional strategies best meet these more rigorous criteria.

Together, students and teachers—working closely with parents, business leaders, social service agencies, and postsecondary institutions—need the opportunity to articulate and reconcile competing customer requirements and the means to address anticipated needs. Only then will students receive the lyrics they deserve: the opportunity and skills to become lifelong learners.

Training on a Shoestring

Because the companies in this study all view training as a critical investment in their human capital, they make certain they provide it. And they do it in ways that prepare employees in advance for the jobs they are expected to assume and the standards they are supposed to meet within the overall context of the organization's goals and objectives. In other words, training is aligned closely with certain tasks or responsibilities that come with the job.

Rarely does the same mindset or resource allocation characterize education. Training in school districts generally is treated as a luxury or afterthought, as flexible dollars often are. And the training, when available, is more ad hoc. Professional development dollars become a way to reward staff rather than improve job performance. In the worst case, training becomes a rite of passage for educators—something to be endured rather than valued and the only way, aside from longevity and assuming extra assignments, to move up the pay schedule. In other words, training in education may result in improved performance, but it is usually through the conscientious efforts of individual participants. Unlike enlightened companies, most school systems (and many companies, for that matter) have not created work processes that link training opportunities specifically to job needs and ultimately to enhancing organizational productivity.

Although the education sites in this study are committed to providing training, they either depend on business to provide it or do it themselves on a shoe string. When, as is the case with TQM, everyone needs training, the lack of training resources and long-term capacity in education are a real dilemma. Most of our sites, in keeping within their budgets, were therefore exploring alternative strategies, such as "train-the-trainer" or "just-in-time" training. However, even these approaches place great pressure on in-house trainers. They must quickly get up to speed to train others on skills they themselves may not yet have fully mastered. Or they must find the time to train others just in time, within the context of having to perform their regular full-time jobs.

Even when educators receive Quality training, it often is at the philosophical level (for example, Deming) or part of a standard methodology (for instance, the Quality tools). Educators rarely receive training in identifying, assessing, realigning, and integrating their own organization's management processes. And they seldom learn how to link such processes to meeting student needs and achieving better results.

No Time

Companies think nothing of scheduling planning meetings or training sessions during the regular work day. Certainly, they do not advocate wasting time, but businesses can use time as they see fit. Some companies may even stop the production line so that their people can be trained or participate in quality action teams.

Time is anything but an afterthought in education. *It is the primary thought.* Finding time for extra activities during the regular school day is, therefore, a real barrier to implementing Quality. Some districts do not have the time, literally, if contract negotiations limit work-related activities to certain hours in the day. Other school systems may encourage their people to meet (or at least not dissuade them from meeting) on their own time, in violation of the contract or hourly wage requirements. In the sites we visited, many teachers and hourly employees were volunteering their own time to participate in Quality training and planning, but this course obviously has its limitations. Although individuals are often willing to make personal sacrifices, no organization (especially one that is trying to build a Quality work environment) wants to "reward" its people by imposing undue burdens on them.

When training for teachers does become available, what do they do with their students? Using substitute teachers becomes a resource allocation issue. Even more critically, it can become an education debit issue as well. In most cases, replacing the regular teacher results in a loss of productivity, as those of us may recall whenever we had the chance to "entertain" a substitute when we were students. If students are not already learning with teams of teachers or in self-managed education settings, using substitutes also forces teachers to make terrible choices—between leaving their classrooms (the primary reason they are in school) and taking advantage of training or planning opportunities. It also becomes difficult to instill the ethos of collaborative decision making when the entire teaching team cannot go off together for training.

The use of time is a real Catch 22 for schools. Administrators who schedule professional development time so that entire schools can participate place a burden on those parents who must find custodial care alternatives for their children. If, on the other hand, school boards add time to the school year so they can provide building staff with training opportunities, it is a cost issue. And finally, no matter how liberally stretched, time is finite. There is just so much to go around. Thus, until TQM becomes the organization's problem-solving strategy (and, as such, is able to empower teams to identify time-saving options), it likely will have to compete with other critical priorities and demands.

No Momentum

The race in business usually belongs to the swift. But companies that become winners also are those with "Big Mo" (for momentum), the tenacity to reach the finish line by sticking with promising ideas long enough to produce results. Thus, leaders in Quality settings, as noted earlier, insist on giving the change process time to germinate, instead of uprooting efforts prematurely and often fatally, in order to evaluate them.

Educators, in contrast, consider themselves lucky when they are even given the chance to cross the starting line. Sustaining a long-term change effort is nearly impossible in education, where leaders, by definition, often get uprooted. If a new person wins an elected official's position, change could mean

starting off in another direction. Raging suboptimization,
fueled in part by the conflicts that often accompany increasing
diversity in our society, makes the challenge of building a lasting consensus even more difficult. Although political turnover
is the price paid for maintaining any democratic society, the lack
of consistent leadership need not be.

Education also is afflicted, in an organizational sense,
with a bias for the short term. Enough fads and programs come
and go that flavor-of-the-*month* might actually be an improvement. The problem is inertia, coupled with an inability to institutionalize promising new practices. Where the typical product
life span in business is eighteen months, in education it is more
likely to be eighteen years. Old ways of doing things are not
replaced because innovations do not stick around long enough
to become common practice. New programs tend to go through
a two- to three-year cycle time for product development, but the
cycle time is zero when it comes to application and replication.
Not many programs make it that far. It is not for lack of trying.
The reasons tend to have more to do with a lack of resources
and evaluation capacity. Many schools and districts are successful at securing external funds to develop new programs. Then
teachers, staff, and administrators invest heavily of their time
and energy in planning the new activities, only to see their
efforts dashed when the funds run out and when commitment
or ability at the district level to sustain the programs is not forthcoming. In addition, many education organizations lack effective evaluation and dissemination processes, so that advocates of
new programs have little nonanecdotal evidence to verify success. As a result, which programs come and go may well rest as
much on district politics (a practice fueled by the rapid turnover
at the top) than on promising practices worth retaining.

Is it any wonder that in such a "system," many teachers
simply shut the doors to their classroom (the ultimate suboptimization), where at least they have some control over activities?
Is it any wonder that many educators respectfully decline the
opportunity for additional training when experience has taught
them that they will not have the same opportunity to apply what
they would have learned? Is it any wonder that innovative principals in some districts may resort to hiding exciting programs

and practices from their district administrators, for fear that the programs, once revealed, will be threatened? Is it any wonder that new initiatives often do not survive the transition when the leaders who sparked them change school buildings or administrative positions? Is it any wonder that in order to learn what is happening, school boards get entangled in management issues when their superintendents, fearing that board members will micromanage, have withheld information? Is it any wonder that students and teachers often get whipsawed between countervailing political forces whenever their district changes course and the drivers are single-issue groups that can decide school board elections because voter turnout is so low? It should not be any wonder, therefore, why constancy of purpose remains a distant promise for some school districts and a cruel joke for most.

Too Much of a Good Thing?

Successful companies empower their people to make decisions in cross-functional teams. Education, because of separate program funding streams and the resulting organizational barriers, often makes its people work in silos. Having toiled in isolation for so long, the silo dwellers (particularly teachers who have been kept apart from other adults) are likely to be totally energized by Quality practices. The opportunity to see one's ideas be taken seriously, come to life, and be enhanced by the contributions of others can be exhilarating. Hence, the temptation is there for TQM to become an end in itself, rather than the change strategy that leads to improving student performance in ways that will satisfy education's multiple customers. This is not through any malice or forethought, but because educators may feel so liberated by working collaboratively that they lose sight of what they are trying to accomplish. As actress Mae West once observed: "Too much of a good thing can be wonderful."

The "good thing"—TQM, in this instance—needs to be tied to results, to improving student and system performance. And it needs to have a management-process focus, so that Quality practices can be tied to real work. Otherwise TQM runs the risk in education circles of being discredited and abandoned, not on its merits, but because of faulty execution. From all that we have observed in conducting this study, such a fate would be a lost opportunity of monumental proportions. And the loss would be borne most by individuals who initially became educators so they could engage their students—their customers— in meaningful learning.

Chapter 7

Advice to Business

Having shared our thoughts on the challenges of implementing TQM in education, we would be remiss if we also did not share some actions business leaders can take to facilitate their involvement. Successful companies can share the benefit of their know-how in implementing Quality with educators who will have to embark on even more taxing journeys to get to the same destination. And they can offer the political shield of their community standing as a way to expand upon and safeguard the journey over time. Consequently, we suggest that companies provide educators with three critical areas of support: *Quality resources,* including training; *management experience* in analyzing management systems and work processes; and *political reinforcement* in building, expanding, and sustaining broad-based change efforts.

Fifteen Action Steps

Business leaders can provide such support by considering fifteen action steps, outlined below:

Advice to Business: Fifteen Action Steps

1. Know thyself.
2. Know thy potential partner.

125

3. Create the infrastructure.
4. Go off site together.
5. Address the big picture.
6. Determine priority areas.
7. Draft a continuous improvement plan and implementation strategy.
8. Prioritize, provide, and promote training.
9. Conduct an organizational assessment.
10. Benchmark: compare best practices.
11. Craft a "Big Mo" strategy.
12. Engage the entire community.
13. Anticipate and head off the glitches.
14. Always ask "Why?"
15. Do unto others.

(For brevity's sake, we refer to "school district" in the sections that follow; however, companies should note that the same assistance is applicable to state departments of education.)

1. Know Thyself

Before offering assistance to educators, it would be wise for companies to conduct an internal assessment of the resources they could furnish. The resources are of five types.

Quality Tools and Processes. District requests for assistance likely will be in using the company's TQM methodology. Thus, business leaders should assess their company's own methodology—that is, the curriculum and tools used in training its own Quality action teams. If more than one company is willing to assist a school district, the responsibility rests with the companies to reconcile for educators their TQM approaches, which except for different terminology should not prove so difficult.

Functional Expertise. Most education sites are likely to need support in defining their management processes before they can track improvements. Therefore, employees who can provide assistance in process design and in specific functions (strategic planning, human resource deployment, and so on), as well as in facilitating group decisions, may be called on to help at different stages. Even successful companies not practicing TQM could play an important support role here.

Leveraging Existing Support. Assistance to educators need not come only from senior managers. Other employees already engaged in supporting more traditional business-education alliances (for example, mentoring students, providing computers, offering skills training to teachers, serving on school-based management teams) also could assist their education partners in using Quality tools, if their companies help make the logical connections for them.

Time Commitment. Companies should be prepared to spend time on assisting school systems. Certainly this includes time in the beginning for planning implementation strategies, but it also may include time for training as well as the time of loaned executives with specific functional expertise. As in any good supplier-customer relationship, this one needs to last *over time* as well.

A Key Contact. For trust to be established between the partners, the partnership needs to stabilize. Thus, business leaders should consider freeing up the services of a senior person who can oversee the work with the district, and, as needed, speak on behalf of and command internal resources from across the company.

Having recommended this last resource, it also should be acknowledged that "loaned executives" can become vulnerable when their own companies restructure. Up-and-coming business leaders, no matter how committed to helping improve education, may be hesitant to spend too much time away from their "real" jobs. Consequently, building internal capacity within education's own ranks to implement TQM may become increasingly important as a change strategy, with businesses playing a more supportive (rather than full-time) role.

2. Know Thy Potential Partner

Before committing to a *continuous* improvement process, companies would be wise to conduct some market analysis on their potential education partner. The partnership with a school district may not be as serious for many as entering into holy matrimony, but it is likely to outlast some marriages. Thus, companies should search out the conditions that most likely will ensure a good match. From what we know about implementing Quality in education, the conditions would include:

- A recognized need and a willingness to change
- A trusting culture
- Stable leadership, or at least a readiness on the part of the school board, superintendent, and employees' unions to come together so they can own the change process
- A vision, mission, and goals (which hopefully have been developed through a collaborative process involving the community) or the willingness to commit to such a process
- A commitment to professional development at all organizational levels
- The willingness and ability to commit time for planning and training activities

A business likely will find that its prospective partner is lacking in one or more of these areas. However, it should still consider working with the district, in order to help create these preconditions for successful implementation.

In an effort to reduce the cycle time of its own learning curve, companies may want to recruit the services of a third party knowledgeable about education, business, and TQM. The third party can play a variety of roles, including conducting an environmental scan of the district's needs and readiness to change; helping the company assess its support base; planting the seeds of organizational cooperation; identifying existing programs and restructuring efforts on which to build; educating key business participants on the cultural and organizational realities of education settings; acting as a temporary bridge between the partners before their relationships are forged; providing strategic interventions, on a recurring basis as needed, to energize and solidify the relationship; and evaluating progress and identifying additional needs.

3. Create the Infrastructure

One of the capacity builders most lacking in education is infrastructure. Individual programs and projects are frequently "managed" by groups that come and go. Therefore, businesses can lend needed aid and comfort to educators by suggesting that they form a *Quality leadership team* to initiate and oversee the change effort. Along with key business leaders, the team should at the very least include representation from the district's education leadership—the school board, the superintendent, and the teachers' and school employees' (nonteaching) unions. Establishing this team is critical to long-term success for several reasons:

Trust. For a successful relationship to be born and survive, the pieces of the education leadership team must envision the change process as a collaborative venture, where information is shared forthrightly and individual priorities are addressed and resolved.

Collective Buy-In. Each of the partners needs to engage the participation and support of critical segments of the population that must be there to make change happen. Board members, as elected officials, must be able to reach out to the community; the superintendent, as the head of the school district, must be able to reach out to all of its employees; and union leaders, as elected representatives, must be able to reach out to their members. The outreach is a two-way process: the leaders need to be able to communicate team decisions to their respective populations as well as reflect their concerns back to the team.

Transitions. Given the frequent turnover at the top in education, if any one or more partners leave, the existence of the team would still position the others—if properly invested—to sustain the effort.

Success. If any of the key education parties mentioned above are left outside of the leadership loop, it is highly unlikely that a long-term change effort can take root, let alone be sustained.

Eventually, Quality practices will need to be rolled out to the entire district, a massive endeavor even in small districts.

Consequently, we suggest strongly that business leaders work with the superintendent to select a Quality executive or staff, reporting directly to the superintendent and the Quality leadership team, whose job it is to design the change strategy, manage the change process, oversee progress, raise emerging issues, and evaluate results.

4. Go Off Site Together

Many of the sites in this study found it essential, in honing their own visions of a future they wished to create, to visit other places. Accordingly, as one of its first activities, the Quality leadership team should consider going off site together to interview individuals and observe activities in a comparable education site that is implementing TQM. Such an initiative should have several benefits:

- *Seeing what is possible.* It is always easier to create a new vision when there is tangible evidence of someone else's vision in practice.
- *Being strategic.* The chance to talk with individuals who are several steps ahead in the change process and observe the results of their efforts should enhance the Quality leadership team's ability to set a direction and plan initial activities.
- *Forging good team relations.* Sharing the experience of going off site and away from normal work pressures should help the team establish an effective working relationship from the start.

5. Address the Big Picture

The big picture should be addressed in several ways.

Build Community Support.   Under the most optimal conditions, a school district will already have articulated its vision, mission, and goals. And education leaders, as a way of reconciling competing customer requirements, will have engaged the community in the process. Only then will community residents likely give educators the time to implement the needed changes. Absent this community template and for all of the reasons stated previously, customizing TQM as a long-term change strategy in education will be more difficult to sustain. Business leaders can help educators create a process, if they have not already done so, that engages the entire community in articulating the district's vision, mission, and goals. If the district already has taken action, business can assist district leaders to translate the goals into measurable objectives and track progress.

   Just-in-Time Training for the Quality Leadership Team and Staff.   Training the Quality leadership team on the use of TQM problem-solving tools would be a real benefit at this stage, for several reasons:

- *Quality of decision making.* Once trained, the team could use the tools in linking goals to actions, identifying problem areas, and coming up with an appropriate course of action. As a result, the substance of team decisions and the subsequent actions are likely to be enhanced.
- *Proof of the benefits.* Demonstrating early on the value of Quality training in decision making should help instill the desire on the part of the district's leadership to continue using the tools and to train others.
- *Creating a collaborative culture.* Using the quality tools at Quality leadership team meetings should help forge a bond among team members and between the district and the company. It also provides opportunities to model desired behaviors.

6. Determine Priority Areas

Before selecting priority areas, business leaders should consider assisting educators in conducting a *baseline study of existing management processes*, using the Baldrige Criteria or an equivalent as a self-assessment tool. The study would enable the Quality leadership team to present TQM as a change strategy that will help the district accomplish existing priorities. Such a strategy also will avoid "project-itis," a common affliction in education, by positioning Quality appropriately as not just another fad or stand-alone project, but the means by which every employee can accomplish organizational and personal goals.

Select Priorities. The opportunity Quality offers education is not in having people work harder necessarily (many educators do that already) but in helping them work smarter. A lot of what people do at work is either unnecessary or unproductive. It has been estimated that only 25 percent of work accomplished in most organizations actually adds value for customers. Business leaders can support educators in making their organizations more efficient and effective. They can assist educators in defining customer needs and in relating work processes and organizational outputs to meeting such needs. Business leaders also can support educators in targeting tight resources on the "critical few" rather than the "trivial many." In the real world of scarcity, such assistance is likely to be welcomed.

As in other organizations, the work performed in education can be aggregated by function, as illustrated in Figure 7.1. Work ranges from the core business of education—the instructional functions (for example, revising curricula or providing staff development)—to the noninstructional functions found in most organizations, such as personnel, budget, planning, or facilities maintenance. (Successful companies that have abandoned their traditional organization charts in favor of overlapping circles and processes should bear with us. This organization chart should be viewed as a starting point, not an endpoint, to enhance business leaders' knowledge of education organizations and point out to educators the opportunities to create cross-functional teams. The purpose of presenting it here is to build a common understanding between business and education.)

Based on district goals, the Quality leadership team should target key work processes, using flowcharts first to track each process and then to improve it. Here are three options, which are not intended to be mutually exclusive:

• *Noninstructional (including administrative) processes.* There are two advantages in working in these areas. First, any cost savings could be spent on district priorities, such as training. Second, the comfort level of business participants is likely to be greater here than in instructional areas, so they will be able to contribute more to the change process. The

Figure 7.1. School System Operations: Key Functions and Work Processes.

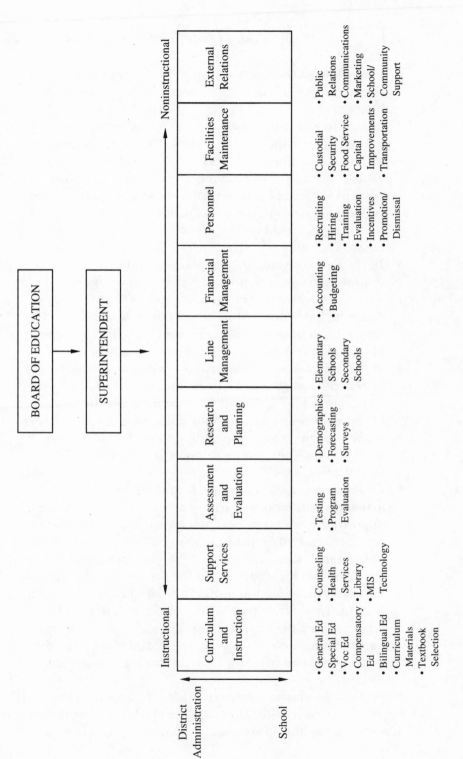

potential disadvantage is that if most district employees and the community do not see "educational" improvements being made as a result of TQM, they may pressure district leaders to abandon the effort. A potential middle ground may be in selecting noninstructional areas that improve the working conditions of the instructional staff so they will still value the results, despite not being intimately involved (except as internal customers) in the deliberations. Examples are improving classroom facilities or cafeteria food, as well as reducing the time it takes to receive supplies or have classroom equipment fixed.

- *Instructional processes.* Quality practices ultimately must improve the key work processes that serve teachers and schools in delivering educational services to children. These include curriculum, instruction, assessment, professional development, and technology. With the exception of the last two work processes, the others are more integral to the business of education and less generic to business in general. But educators, once trained in the use of TQM, also could figure out how to customize the tools for education-specific decisions. Improving these processes is likely to have a great payoff by ensuring that the work of all those employees who want to be student focused is student focused.

- *Classroom management processes.* If students are to become managers of their own learning processes, they need the opportunity to learn how. Therefore, while the district is concentrating on improving the overall work processes of the system, it should simultaneously consider providing opportunities for students and their teachers to be trained in Quality practices and tools. This last strategy also could have the most immediate impact, much as it did in Mt. Edgecumbe, where parents, teachers, administrators, and the community could witness a significant change for the better in student behavior and ultimately performance.

Consider Time and Training Needs.　In selecting functional or process areas in which to work, the Quality leadership team also should use the TQM tools to determine two other issues:

first, how best to use *time* in engaging participants in training and planning activities; and second, how best to provide the *training* (in cross-functional teams or by family unit; cascaded or piloted, and so on). Obviously, the answers should be determined by the intended outcomes and existing conditions within each district. However, it would be wise when selecting priorities to include a discussion of these issues. (See below for some additional thoughts on training.)

Help Make Systemic Change Systemic. There may be a temptation for the Quality leadership team to work at the school level, ignoring the district administration. Change is often easier when there is the chance to create a new school, as we witnessed in Prince William County and Millcreek Township. And change may be more fun to implement at the elementary school level, when faculty are not constrained by subject matter silos (and the primary customers are often cuter).

Business leaders are not alone if they prefer to work at the school level. Some leading education restructuring advocates also have given up on school districts as viable change agents. They believe that the only way to restructure education is one school at a time, by building a self-empowering culture within. If the school board and district administration remain outside the loop, however, long-term change becomes less likely. All too often, unfortunately, when building leaders leave, the positive changes they have initiated do not survive the transition. Thus, if a district is inclined to pilot TQM at the school level, business leaders should work with the Quality leadership team to *broaden the efforts* at least to include more than one school *and* those district administrators who work most closely with the schools.

It is also not surprising that business leaders want to focus their energies on improving "results" in education. After all, a similar focus has enabled them to stay in business. Many education restructuring advocates also are attempting to focus on results by developing more rigorous student achievement standards (subject matter, skills-based, or performance standards). Many of these advocates demonstrate little patience for "process" and change management issues, considerations that tend to slow up the changes. Absent an appreciation for "process," however, they also lack the means to assist educators in achieving higher standards once they have been developed. Business leaders who have experienced successes with TQM can introduce Quality into the change mix, so that "process" becomes not a dirty word or an excuse for inaction, but the strategic means to accomplish the results everyone so eagerly awaits.

7. Draft a Continuous Improvement Plan and Implementation Strategy

If TQM ultimately is to become a systemic change strategy, there needs to be a *continuous improvement plan.* Businesses can help the Quality leadership team formulate a plan that actually results in action and enables members to track improvements over time. A plan also will help target the effort on achieving priorities and give it a needed focus within the district and the community. If the community understands what is ahead, it should be more inclined to support the effort over time. Here are some additional issues to consider:

Chunking.   Based on our findings in the sites, we suggest selecting priorities, but in *manageable chunks,* to be able to demonstrate some early successes. Initial results need not be limited to performance; they can be behavioral as well. Tracking short-term behavioral changes (a Quality action team's ability to function effectively, eliminating unnecessary decision points in a process) are important in and of themselves. And they also can help buy needed time for performance results to eventually kick in.

Soft Stuff, Hard Stuff, or Both?   Based on the experience of the companies and education sites in this study, an approach to TQM based on the "soft stuff"—an organizational development model—needs to precede the "hard stuff"—statistical process controls. Trust needs to be established first within the education system, as well as between education and business, before progress can be measured. Ultimately, however, both the soft stuff and the hard stuff need to be there, so that educators are able to track progress. If educators know "what works," they can tell others, thereby guarding their management prerogatives without being crisis-driven and always having others telling them what to do. Information is power, as is the ability to make decisions.

Do You Name It? Some of the sites in this study named their Quality initiative in order to provide a focus to the change efforts. Others selected a more low-key approach, so that likely opponents or skeptics would not have as obvious a target. This is a judgment call, given the particular setting, that business—by raising the issue—can help educators make.

Realignment. Once educators begin to implement Quality, they soon realize that their management processes need to be realigned in order to identify and meet customer requirements as well as to build a trusting, collaborative culture that will serve all customers well. Business leaders can assist educators in designing incentives (and removing disincentives in the current system) that will reinforce and reward desired behaviors. They can help ensure input from key parties—such as unions and parents—in identifying and implementing appropriate incentives. And they can support educators in crafting suitable Quality incentives for managers regarding their evaluations and promotions.

8. Prioritize, Provide, and Promote Training

Unilateral training is a luxury in education. The resources are not there, consequently, educators are often totally dependent on outside—usually business—support for TQM training. In determining what types of training would make the most sense, here are some issues to think about.

Capitalize on What Educators Know and Do. Education, after all, is a "learning enterprise." Educators, by definition, should already be trained to engage others in the learning process. Therefore, many educators may have received training previously in interpersonal skills development, running meetings, and so on—some of the essential components of TQM. In formulating effective training strategies, it therefore makes sense to survey the customer and find out what training does not have to be duplicated. It also makes good business sense, both in saving (cycle) time and cost, as well as in meeting customer needs by providing what is missing, not what is already there.

Enhance the Odds for Application. Given the lack of training resources in education and also the need for opportunities to *apply* training soon after delivery, businesses should help educators in using training resources strategically. One potential model would be to provide just-in-time training for people who will be addressing the priorities identified in the continuous improvement plan, and then work with them to apply the training to improving their work processes.

Train Instructional Staff. TQM still is depicted in most education circles as a "management thing"—something that only administrators do. Teachers, however, are managers where it counts most: in the classroom. If the ultimate goal of changing the education system is to improve student performance, students eventually must assume responsibility for their own individual continuous improvement plans. The best way for a school district to institutionalize Quality capacity is to train its teachers, who also tend to stay in place longer than both administrators and (hopefully) students. In addition, teachers often are the customers of the products administrators develop. They need to be involved as well in the key administrative decisions that influence what they do in the classroom.

Help Build a Long-Term Training Capacity. Just as implementation of Quality practices is continuous, so also are training needs. People change jobs and need new skills. Job requirements change, and people in those jobs have to be retrained. Business, based on its own experiences, can assist educators in several important respects:

- *Train the trainers.* Companies can help train education staff on the TQM tools and decision-making processes. The district will then have a cadre of its own trainers to provide support to the various units implementing Quality.
- *Open up existing corporate training to educators.* Make training slots in Quality classes available to educators on an ongoing basis. Not only will such courses provide a consistent and sorely needed resource to educators; they also will help forge an ongoing partnership, where each party can learn in class from the unique experiences of others.
- *Assess the value of training.* Companies can help educators assess the impact of training on improving job performance, as well as in identifying what skills will be needed by people to perform these jobs.
- *Engage other key suppliers in improving training.* Most educators, in order to gain salary steps or receive certification as

administrators, have to earn continuing education credits.
The suppliers of this training usually are *local institutions of
higher education*, as well as the *professional education associations*
that sponsor conferences for credit. Companies can help
educators work with their suppliers to leverage these existing training opportunities on improving job performance.
And they can encourage higher education institutions to
offer TQM training as well as integrate the teaching of Quality practices into their regular curricula. The natural course
of supply and demand should act as a strong motivator that
encourages education suppliers to move in this direction,
particularly if their key customers—local companies and
school districts—promote such initiatives through their own
hiring and in-service preferences.

- *Institutionalize capacity.* Companies can work with educators,
as businesses have done in Jefferson County (Louisville)
and Cincinnati to create professional development acade-
mies. They can be effective advocates on behalf of using
public (as well as foundation and corporate) funds to build
a long-term training entity with capacity that serves district
needs subsequent to initial Quality training.

- *Advocate training.* Based on their own investments, successful companies are well positioned to make the case for
training as one—if not *the*—essential element in improving education. Business leaders, through their own experiences, can educate public officials and the public at large
on the value of and need for such expenditures.

- *Help make training respectable.* Training is essential when TQM
is being implemented because everyone changes roles and
responsibilities—or at least the way they execute those
responsibilities. Therefore, in the spirit of continuous
improvement, everyone, including school board members
and superintendents, will need training. Such thoughts
might be expected to occur naturally in a learning enterprise, but admitting to a need for training may be perceived
by some as a weakness, rather than an opportunity to
improve. Training also may be viewed as a bother by busy
people. (Based on the past experiences of many education
professionals, such a reaction is not unreasonable.) Because
of their own experiences with and commitment to training,

however, enlightened companies can make a compelling case on its behalf.

• *Help make training possible.* Having everyone engage in common training opportunities also can help eliminate the functional silos across and up and down education organizations, as well as across various community entities. By providing or participating in the training, business can invite all the key players to the party.

9. Conduct an Organizational Assessment

The seven Baldrige Categories (or comparable Quality criteria) are powerful tools in helping organizations improve themselves. They also provide a common language whereby representatives of different institutions can pool their respective areas of expertise in conducting self-assessments. Business, for example, can lend expertise in conducting an organizational assessment, as well as in analyzing the work processes that connect specific functional areas. Educators can contribute their firsthand expertise on school system operations in general and the meshing of needs, priorities, culture, personalities, roles, and relationships of their own organizations in particular.

In addition to starting the change process, an assessment can provide the momentum to keep it going, by identifying opportunities for improvement on an ongoing basis. If the assessment tracks district goals and priorities, the results can be a *valid, useful report card to the community*, which the Quality leadership team can use to identify priorities, demonstrate progress, and request community support in addressing emerging needs. By acting as a political buffer, business also can help educators reconcile, in a constructive fashion, any differences between their supplier specifications and the customer requirements coming from the community.

10. Benchmark: Compare Best Practices

Educators are hungry for resources—certainly training and funding, but also ideas and information. Identifying the sources of good practices can help education leaders build their own data base. Training educators on how to benchmark can help them improve their own work processes. Several additional considerations follow.

Expect Some Initial Resistance.   Grades traditionally have been used to sort and rank students and schools into what amounts to winners and losers, as have SAT scores and dropout rates at the district level. The rankings have significant ramifications, not only on the self-esteem of children, but also on the value, literally in the case of real estate values, placed on neighborhoods. Consequently, it is understandable that educators, when first exposed to benchmarking, may be leery. Once they understand the purpose of benchmarking, however, increasing numbers of educators become excited about the potential opportunity to "learn from the best," not only from education, but also from other public and private sectors, including their business partners. As the suppliers of business, educators also need to see how their customers track their own processes.

Compare Companywide Efforts at Different Sites.   Companies that are working with educators to implement Quality in different locations can benchmark the experiences and results of such activities as a way to improve initiatives at all sites. Similarly, different companies can also benchmark their education activities.

Puncture Community Complacency.   Benchmarking also could have an important side benefit. It could empower educators to deal with community self-satisfaction, by helping the community see the need for change.   Demonstrating that another organization does things better may be an appropriate salve to cure the "my school is fine, thank you very much" ailment. However, businesses also should be prepared to stand by educators who are brave enough to puncture their community's balloon.

National Implications.   Bolstered by the Baldrige Award, all sorts of companies are benchmarking against the Baldrige winners and other successful companies so that all boats captained by the captains of American industry can rise in a competitive global marketplace. And many successful companies are more than willing, and in fact eager, to share successful practices with others, even competitors, as a way of goading themselves to improve.

Applying the same mindset to education by benchmarking effective work processes (as well as efforts to achieve the Six
National Education Goals, implement The Business Roundtable's Nine Essential Components of a Successful Education
System,[1] or ensure that all students can meet increasingly
higher education standards) is likely to have a comparable positive impact nationally and internationally.

11. Craft a "Big Mo" Strategy

When change strategies are crafted, participants tend to concentrate first on goals and next on an implementation strategy,
ignoring the concurrent need to craft a communication strategy. In the public sector, as much thought needs to be devoted
to *keeping everyone routinely informed of what is going on* as to what
is going on, if for no other reason than to buy time to do what
needs doing.

Business leaders should tread into education waters
knowing how to swim against the tide. They need to recognize
how difficult sharing information is likely to be in an environment where competing constituencies need to be served and
articulation of problems frequently results in open warfare. For
improvements to happen, bad news must be shared, not sup-
pressed. And coalitions, which are often prickly, must stay
together. How the news is reported to the community will likely have a great impact on what does or does not happen as a con-
sequence. Business leaders can play a critical support role by
ensuring that their colleagues in the business community, as
well as the media, are routinely informed on "the root causes"
underlying potentially heated issues.

Motorola conceived of what it calls the *4 I's of cultural
change* to outline the stages of any change process. The same
characteristics that apply to training people can be applied to
entire systems:

• *Inspiration.* To accept doing something new, people and
  organizations need to embrace the benefits of changing.

---

[1] See Appendix C for a list of the National Education Goals and The Business Roundtable's Nine Points.

- *Information.* To move away from the status quo to the preferred state, people and organizations need to understand what they are doing and why.
- *Implementation.* To make the necessary changes, people and organizations need tools and resources to achieve the intended results.
- *Institutionalization.* For the change initiative to extend beyond a one-time effort, people and organizations need to have initial efforts reinforced.

Recognizing that the school district is likely to encounter the 4 I's, the Quality leadership team needs to include specific strategies that anticipate each I and that can sustain the effort through institutionalization in its continuous improvement plan.

Business can help educators devise successful strategies for the long term. Several strategies (self-assessments, benchmarking) have already been discussed. Additional strategies could include *periodic surveys and interviews* of internal and external customers designed to gauge their place on the 4 I's continuum as well as to identify any potential barriers (and enablers). South Carolina, since it enacted its first major education reform package in 1984, has distributed annual report cards throughout the state and nationally on "what the penny (increase in the sales tax) has earned" by way of increased student achievements and other improvement indicators. Similarly, businesses can help educators develop *effective communication strategies* to inform their communities of progress and problems.

12. Engage the Entire Community

Business leaders can help bring to the table all the key community stakeholders. They can engage key institutions that are both customers and suppliers of the school system—higher education, local agencies, unions, other companies, and government leaders—in improving services directed to the same customers, parents and their children. TQM could become an effective communitywide strategy in dealing with shared problems, especially when the full impact of education's failures does not show up as costs until later in another segment of the community (prisons, welfare). These realities make a compelling argument for all community entities to join forces in reducing cycle time and eliminating defects in each part of the system that serves community residents.

Quality companies also can devise strategies to roll out TQM to other important community sectors—other companies, small and large; the health care industry, where interest in Quality is growing; and two-year and four-year colleges, which can provide the long-term training ground on Quality for the entire community. The more institutions are engaged in the same decision-making processes, the more likely that Quality change efforts will be sustained, and more important, that it will produce good decisions on behalf of the entire community.

Business leaders can provide a real public service by encouraging community leaders to use Quality practices at the policymaking levels. They can assist community stakeholders in understanding the meaning and substantial price paid both in effectiveness and efficiency when organizations suboptimize their priorities. TQM tools also should help community leaders develop the capacity to address constructively the very legitimate questions raised by diversity. Business leaders can initiate community collaboratives (such as the Erie Excellence Council), and they can sustain them. They can bring institutions to the table and keep them there, particularly as key community leaders come and go. Finally, business leaders can help create realistic expectations within the community and buy educators the time needed to make real change happen. The cycle time for most students is thirteen years (from kindergarten through grade twelve). Therefore, decisions made in the early grades may not demonstrate their worth until years later, in the career choices made by students and even in something as basic as whether they decide to stay in school at all. Business leaders can help make public expectations more realistic, while simultaneously providing an impetus for needed changes to occur.

13. Anticipate and Head Off the Glitches

The bedrock of TQM is anticipating problems before they appear. Businesses can assist educators in doing the same. Some of the likely issues that will need to be addressed are touched on below.

Transitions. Assuming in advance that some of the original partners of the Quality leadership team are likely to turn
over, companies should build linkages to likely successors (if
known) and their institutions (which are known) so that new
people will not derail the ongoing change effort but will instead
be given the chance to add constructively to it.

Replenish. Companies should consider sponsoring an
evaluation after three years into the change process, which
seems to be a critical time when organizations may hit a wall of
resistance prior to changes taking root. The results should provide momentum for subsequent actions. In addition, the Quality leadership team should recruit new players in the change
process and new processes to work on, in the effort to replenish, broaden, and sustain the change effort.

Equity. In equal partnerships, the partners obviously
have to be equal. Consequently, companies should seek out
opportunities to support educators in becoming equal partners
in a potential continuous improvement effort, by having *them*
train and advise other organizations. Not only is this wise for the
obvious egalitarian reason; it also makes good business sense.
As long as educators are viewed as the less fortunate, more
needy partner, they are likely to stay that way. If business leaders want to play a more supportive rather than all encompass-
ing role in assisting educators (a growing reality as increasing
numbers of companies are reassessing staff responsibilities
based on bottom-line decisions), they should work with educators to identify opportunities that will enhance the latter
group's self-sufficiency and community status.

14. Always Ask "Why?"

One of the best features of Quality is its insistence on identifying the "root cause" of problems. In working with education systems, business leaders are advised to keep the same perspective.
Always ask "why?" What they see in education organizations may
at first seem strange until the root cause is discovered. In irrational systems (such as the one described in the "Perils" section
of Chapter Six), a lot of behavior appears irrational, when in
truth, it is very rational behavior in reaction to irrational work
processes and conditions.

For example, teachers who shut their classroom doors and decline training and collaborative decision-making opportunities or technology that would benefit their students appear irrational. But their behavior becomes understandable when one learns the root cause of such actions—their previous negative experiences with collaborative planning or training, or their lack of training on using the technology. In point of fact, given the conditions in the education system, closing their doors may be the most rational act that teachers could perform. Unfortunately, the results, in missed opportunities for teachers and their students, are not.

Often what business leaders encounter from educators may appear to be an overemphasis on "process," defensiveness, or resistance, when, in fact, it is the need to engage other people in the decisions, a lack of familiarity or resources, or sheer trepidation of the unknown. Using Quality tools to determine the root cause of resistance and identify appropriate solutions should assist educators in becoming more focused and more effective in making their system rational. When confronted with seemingly irrational behaviors, it would be understandable (and certainly rational) for businesses to simply throw in the towel. But those are precisely the times when root cause analysis needs to be employed in staying the course.

15. Do Unto Others

Business leaders need to be realistic about how long it takes to implement TQM, particularly given the organizational and political context of education. At the same time, they should not be hesitant to support (in a supportive way, of course) higher standards and a strategic focus to the change efforts. Their value added to educators, as thoughtful and politically astute education leaders are the first to acknowledge and encourage, is in pushing for change. External pressures give educators the cover they may need in driving the internal reforms.

Business leaders, in seeking to support educators, should apply the same judgment, commitment, restraint, and expectations that they used in reinventing their own companies. Much like they do with their own employees—and should with their employees who devote time and energy to improving education—they also need to *celebrate educators who make a difference.*

A Concluding Observation

As Paul Allaire, CEO of Xerox Corporation, observed: "Sales reps [read: teachers] want to satisfy the customer [read: student] otherwise they wouldn't go into sales [read: education.] They always have the right attitude. The system is what screws it up. The purpose of the quality process is to fix the system above them."[2]

Most educators enter the field of education because they want to work with young people. Sometimes their intentions and ability get lost along the way. In trying to "fix the system above them," we need to focus on why.

In suggesting TQM as a systemic change strategy in education, we make two basic assumptions. First, virtually all people would rather do a good job at their job than a bad job. Second, the best experts on the problems with any job are usually the people who are trying to do the job. Thus, in fixing the system, we need to be sure to seek and act on their input. The education and business leaders cited in this study are courageous pathfinders and worthy role models. One purpose of capturing their activities in this book has been to reinforce their ranks by prompting comparable initiatives from others.

If we have done a credible job as suppliers, our "product" has delivered three strong messages:

1. Companies practicing TQM have a *valuable resource* to share with educators.
2. Quality *can* work as a systemic change strategy to redesign education.
3. Whether Quality *will* work, however, depends on educators being able to overcome substantial barriers, which they are not likely to be able to do *unless business helps.*

---

[2] Comments in brackets added by authors.

This book has attempted to show why and to suggest how.

Change involves a leap of faith, like the trapeze artist who lets go of the first bar only when a higher bar is visibly within her grasp. Absent the second bar and the ability to grab it, most people choose—and with good reason—to stay where they are. In an effort to improve, all types of organizations are encouraging their employees to aim for the higher bar. Business, government, and education leaders are recognizing the need to empower their people to work together at every level. Just as critically, however, they need to provide their people with support systems that will enable them to succeed.

Changes such as those contemplated in these pages will take time, but time is running out. Education leaders need to be given the opportunity to redesign school systems. And business leaders need to be right there alongside them to offer support, encouragement, and cutting-edge common sense.

Appendix A

Education Sites
Demographic Profiles

Rappahannock County Public Schools, Sperryville, Virginia

- Superintendent:
  Dr. David M. Gangel
  Box 273
  Sperryville, VA 22740
  703/987-8773
- 1,108 students
  —6% minority
  —Socioeconomic diversity from wealthy to poor; horse
  farms to artists' communes
  —17.5% eligible for free and reduced lunch program
- Two schools: one elementary school (K–7), one high school
  (8–12)
- Approximately 130 employees (3 administrators in central
  office)
- FY 1992 budget: $4.8 million

Prince William County Public Schools, Manassas, Virginia

- Superintendent:
  Dr. Edward L. Kelly

P.O. Box 389
Manassas, VA 22110
703/791-8712
* 44,000 students
  —Third largest district in the state
  —23% minority (17% African American, 5% Hispanic,
  1–2% Asian) Transient population in parts of the
  county (in some schools, 40% of students may not have
  started in the school building in which they finished
  the year)
* Sixty-one schools: thirty-nine elementary schools, eleven
  middle schools, seven secondary schools, three special
  education schools, one alternative school
  —Nine new schools in the past five years
* Approximately 7,500 employees
* FY 1992 budget: over $300 million

Mt. Edgecumbe High School, Sitka, Alaska

* Superintendent:
  Todd Bergman (1993–1994)
  1330 Seward Avenue
  Sitka, AK 99835
  907/966-2201
* Approximately 250 students
  —High school (9–12)
  —Opened as a boarding school in 1947 by the Bureau
  of Indian Affairs (BIA). In 1983, the BIA closed the
  school. Reopened by the state of Alaska in 1985.
  Curriculum includes emphasis on Pacific Rim
  studies
  —Public boarding school, available to all high school–
  aged state residents but targeted to Alaska's rural
  students
  —87% minority from eleven different ethnic groups
* One school
* Twenty professional staff (maintenance, dormitory aids,
  and food workers are contractual)
* FY 1992 budget: $6 million

School District of Beloit Turner, Beloit, Wisconsin

- Superintendent:
  Dr. Charles A. Melvin III
  1231 Inman Parkway
  Beloit, WI 53511
  608/362-0771
- 5,500 students
  —4.5% minority
  —Suburban community with manufacturing emphasis
  —5.7% eligible for free and reduced lunch program
- Four schools: two elementary (K–2, 3–5) schools, one
  middle school, one high school
- 176 total employees (3 administrators in central office)
- FY 1992 budget: $6.1 million

Brodhead School District, Brodhead, Wisconsin

- Superintendent:
  Dr. Steven M. Ashmore
  P.O. Box 258
  Brodhead, WI 53520
  608/897-2141
- 5,500 students
  —Rural, small town, manufacturing and farming
  community
  —2.4% minority
  —17% eligible for free and reduced lunch program
- Three schools: one elementary school (K–5), one middle
  school (6–8), one high school (9–12)
- 147 total employees (3 administrators in central office)
- FY 1992 budget: $6 million

Oregon School District, Oregon, Wisconsin

- Superintendent:
  Dr. Linda K. Barrows
  200 No. Main Street
  Oregon, WI 53575
  608/835-3161

- 2,500 students
  —Rural, small town/suburban, manufacturing and farming community
  —1.5% minority
  —6% eligible for free and reduced lunch program
- Five schools: two elementary schools (K–3, K–6), one middle school (4–6), one junior high school (7–8), one high school (9–12)
- 311 total employees (4 administrators in central office)
- FY 1992 budget: $6 million

Parkview School District, Orfordville, Wisconsin

- Superintendent:
  Dr. David Romstad
  106 W. Church Street
  Orfordville, WI 53576
  608/879-2352
- 4,500 students
  —Rural, small town, primarily farming community
  —1.5% minority
  —18% eligible for free and reduced lunch program
- Four schools: three elementary schools (K–6), one junior high/senior high school (7–12)
- 173 total employees (3 administrators in central office)
- FY 1992 budget: $7.2 million

Pecatonica School District, Pecatonica, Wisconsin

- Superintendent:
  Ms. Nancy Hendrickson
  P.O. Box 117
  Pecatonica, WI 53516
  608/523-4248
- 525 students
  —Rural
  —0.5% minority
  —14% eligible for free and reduced lunch program

- Two schools: one elementary school (K–6), one high school (7–12)
- 75 total employees (3 administrators)
- FY 1992 budget: $2.9 million

Vermont Department of Education, Montpelier

- Commissioner:
  Dr. Richard P. Mills
  120 State Street
  Montpelier, VT 05620-2501
  802/828-3135
- 251 school districts
- Serves over 100,000 children and adult students
  throughout the state
  —2.4% minority students
  —25% eligible for free and reduced lunch program
- 132 employees in K–12 services, organized in
  "home teams"
- FY 1992 budget: $679.4 million

George Westinghouse Vocational and Technical High School, Brooklyn, New York

- Principal:
  Mr. Lewis A. Rappaport
  105 Johnson Street
  Brooklyn, NY 11201
  708/625-6130
- 1,700 students
  —74% African American, 23% Hispanic
  —25% female
  —Over 60% eligible for free and reduced lunch
  program
  —Many from single-parent, low-income families
- One high school (9–12); citywide magnet school
- Over 150 total employees
- FY 1992 budget: $5.8 million

The Erie Community

Millcreek Township Public Schools

- Superintendent:
  Robert J. Agnew
  Millcreek Education Center
  3740 West 26th Street
  Erie, PA 16506
  814/835-5300
- Approximately 7,500 students
  —Surrounds Erie on three sides; agricultural and manufac-
    turing community
  —1.5% eligible for free and reduced lunch program
- Twelve schools: seven elementary schools, four middle
  schools (one opened in fall 1993), one intermediate
  high school (9–10), one senior school (11–12)
- Approximately 700 total employees (11 administrators in
  central office)
- FY 1992 budget: $41.5 million

World Center for Community Excellence

- Erie Excellence Council
  1006 State Street
  Erie, PA 16501
  814/456-9223

Appendix B

Additional Resources

Publications on Quality and Elementary and Secondary Education

American Association of School Administrators. *Creating Quality Schools*. Arlington, Va.: American Association of School Administrators, 1992. 34 pp.

Bonstingl, John Jay. *Schools of Quality: An Introduction to Total Quality Management in Education*. Alexandria, Va.: Association for Supervision and Curriculum Development, 1992. 109 pp.

Bradley, Leo H. *Total Quality Management for Schools*. Lancaster, Pa.: Technomic Publishing Company, 1993. 215 pp.

Byrnes, Margaret A., Cornesky, Robert A., and Byrnes, Lawrence W. *The Quality Teacher: Implementing Total Quality Management in the Classroom*. Port Orange, Fla.: Cornesky and Associates Press, 1992. 338 pp.

McCormick, Betty L. (ed.). *Quality & Education: Critical Linkages*. Princeton Junction, N.J.: Eye on Education, 1993. 312 pp.

Schenkat, Randy. *Quality Connections: Transforming Schools Through Total Quality Management*. Alexandria, Va.: Association for Supervision and Curriculum Development, 1993. 103 pp.

Other Resources Pertaining to Quality in Education

Networks

- *The Total Quality Network* provides an information and
  shared learning exchange for leaders concerned with systemic, continuous improvement in the quality of school
  outcomes and processes. Materials include seminars, publications, the Deming library of videotapes of Quality in education, a *TQM Handbook* (which converts the 1992 Baldrige
  Criteria into education terminology), and a directory of
  network members by state.

  American Association of School Administrators
  1801 North Moore Street
  Arlington, VA 22209-9988
  703/528-0700

Quality Methodology and Tools for Educators

- *The Koalaty Kid Manual* describes a systematic process
  for achieving desired outcomes and continuous improvement with elementary school students. Activities involve
  a team approach, including teachers, administrators,
  students, parents, volunteers, and business partners. First
  piloted in 1988, the manual was produced in cooperation
  with Corning, Inc. and the American Society for Quality
  Control.

  ASQC
  611 E. Wisconsin Avenue
  P.O. Box 3005
  Milwaukee, WI 53201-3005
  800/248-1946

- *The Memory Jogger for Education: A Pocket Guide of Tools for
  Continuous Improvement in Schools* provides information on
  the philosophy of continuous improvement and problem-
  solving/graphic techniques. It includes seven graphic techniques useful for analysis and display of numerical data in

problem-solving and process improvement efforts. The techniques are the following: Cause and Effect Diagram, Flowchart, Pareto Chart, Run Chart, Histogram, Check Sheet, Control Chart, Scatter Diagram, and so on. Also available is a *Glossary of Terms*, a list of Quality terms for educators, and a *Total Quality Management in Education* videotape series.

GOAL/QPC
13 Branch Street
Methuen, MA 01844
508/685-3900

- *Total Quality Transformation®* is a comprehensive training system that supports organizations in their quality improvement activities, with supplements for educators. Included are foundations (theory and examples) for leaders and for teams, team-based system improvement process, tools, and train-the-trainer seminars.

Productivity-Quality Systems, Inc.
P.O. Box 750010
Dayton, OH 45475-0010
800/777-3020

Quality Methodology Based on Private Sector Experiences

- *Leadership Through Quality* are resource materials published by Xerox. Compiled from the corporation's own implementation of Quality, it is now sold to the public. Included are materials on developing interactive skills, Quality processes and tools, concepts of Quality, the problem-solving process, and benchmarking techniques.

Xerox Customer Parts and Product Support Center
Building 214-07S
P.O. Box 1020
Webster, NY 14580
ATT: Customer Service Lead
1-800-828-5881

- *The Malcolm Baldrige National Quality Award Criteria* represents an organizational self-assessment tool that is updated annually by the Quality Award Office. Also available are case studies of company applications and materials on *Designing and Implementing a State Quality Award,* including a directory of existing state programs.

The Malcolm Baldrige National Quality Award
U.S. Department of Commerce
Technology Administration
National Institute of Standards and Technology
Route 270 and Quince Orchard Road
Administration Building, Room A537
Gaithersburg, MD 20899
301/975-2036

Appendix C

Points, Goals, and Essential Components

The reader is likely to note that the Six National Education Goals, The Business Roundtable's Nine Essential Components, and Deming's Fourteen Points are not always compatible. Because so many educators who are implementing Quality begin with a grounding in Deming's principles, these discrepancies should prompt a healthy debate about the purpose of American education among American business, government, and education leaders. Hopefully, the outcome of that discussion will lead to positive actions, using Quality to improve the education system.

W. Edwards Deming's Fourteen Points

1. Create constancy of purpose for improvement of product and service.
2. Adopt the new philosophy.
3. Cease dependence on mass inspection.
4. End the practice of awarding business on price tag alone.
5. Improve constantly and forever the system of production and service.
6. Institute training.
7. Institute leadership.

8. Drive out fear.
9. Break down barriers between staff areas.
10. Eliminate slogans, exhortations, and targets for the workforce.
11. Eliminate numerical quotas.
12. Remove barriers to pride of workmanship.
13. Institute a vigorous program of education and training.
14. Take action to accomplish the transformation.[1]

The Six National Education Goals

1. By the year 2000, all children in America will start school ready to learn.
2. By the year 2000, the high school graduation rate will increase to at least 90 percent.
3. By the year 2000, American students will leave grades four, eight, and twelve having demonstrated competency in challenging subject matter, including English, mathematics, science, history, and geography; and every school in America will ensure that all students learn to use their minds well, so they may be prepared for responsible citizenship, further learning, and productive employment in our modern economy.
4. By the year 2000, U.S. students will be first in the world in science and mathematics achievement.
5. By the year 2000, every adult American will be literate and will possess the knowledge and skills necessary to compete in a global economy and exercise the rights and responsibilities of citizenship.
6. By the year 2000, every school in America will be free of drugs and violence and will offer a disciplined environment conducive to learning.

The Business Roundtable Education Public Policy Agenda: Nine Essential Components of a Successful Education System

1. The new system is committed to four operating assumptions:

[1]Reprinted by permission of The Putnam Publishing Group from *The Deming Management Method* by Mary Walton. Copyright © 1986 by Mary Walton.

- All students can learn at significantly higher levels.
- We know how to teach all students successfully.
- Curriculum content must reflect high expectations for all students, but instructional time and strategies may vary to assure success.
- Every child must have an advocate.

2. The new system is performance or outcome based.
3. Assessment strategies must be as strong and rich as the outcomes.
4. Schools should receive rewards for success, assistance to improve, and penalties for failure.
5. School-based staff have a major role in making instructional decisions.
6. Major emphasis is placed on staff development.
7. A high-quality prekindergarten program is established, at least for all disadvantaged students.
8. Health and other social services are sufficient to reduce significant barriers to learning.
9. Technology is used to raise student and teacher productivity and to expand access to learning.

Index

Reader Feedback Survey
The National Alliance of Business • Center for Excellence in Education

Please complete this form after you have had the opportunity to read *Using Quality to Redesign School Systems*. The information will be used to evaluate and improve our products and services.

Name: _____ Title: _____

Organization: _____

Address: _____ City: _____

State: _____ Zip Code: _____

Phone: _____ Fax: _____

We would appreciate knowing how you learned about *Using Quality to Redesign School Systems*.

❑ Advertisement   ❑ My Organization
❑ Bookstore   ❑ Gift
❑ Friend or Associate   ❑ Radio or TV Interviews
❑ Library   ❑ Newspaper/Magazine Article
❑ Conference Presentation   ❑ Other (please specify)

Background:
❑ Business   ❑ School Administrator
❑ Government   ❑ University Professor
❑ Teacher   ❑ Student
❑ Parent   ❑ Other (please specify)

Does your organization practice Total Quality Management?
❑ Yes   ❑ No

How would you rate the contents of this book:
❑ Excellent   ❑ Good   ❑ Fair   ❑ Poor

How helpful did you find each section of this book:

	Not at All Helpful	Somewhat Helpful	Very Helpful
Explanation of TQM (Chapter 2)			❑
TQM: Case studies in business and education (Chapter 3)		❑	❑
Analysis of implementation strategies (Chapter 4)	❑	❑	❑
Education applications of TQM (Chapter 5)	❑	❑	❑
Analysis of the education system (Chapter 6)	❑	❑	❑
Advice to business leaders (Chapter 7)	❑	❑	❑

How do you plan to use this book?
❑ Share with others to increase their awareness of TQM
❑ Begin a TQM effort in my organization
❑ Enhance the TQM effort in my organization
❑ Benchmark practices
❑ Support educators to implement TQM
❑ I do not plan to use this book
❑ Other (please specify)

We would welcome any additional comments and suggestions you may have. Please call the **Center for Excellence in Education** at (202) 289-2923. Thank you for your feedback.

cut out page and fold here

Dr. Peggy Siegel
Center for Excellence in Education
National Alliance of Business
1201 New York Avenue, NW, Suite 700
Washington, D.C. 20005-3917